AF679123

SEARCH AND SEIZURE, THE POLICE OFFICER PATROLLING WITHIN THE FOURTH AMENDMENT

By

Flavio Mota, Attorney

First Edition

773-304-6686

fmota4@aol.com

ISBN 978-0-615-8609-09

TABLE OF CONTENTS

Preface

This book combines law enforcement theory with application to deliver the practical aspects of Search and Seizure law (commonly referred to as Stop and Frisk Law); this book is ideal for law enforcement academies. (The main topic of this book is Criminal Procedure the Investigatory Process.) Additionally, this writing can be used as the primary book or as a supplement. Moreover, this instrument is an excellent tool for colleges and universities. This book gives the student a deep understanding of the complex laws that regulate law enforcement officers.

What separates this book from other sources is the combination of theory and practice. This means that the student (whether in college or in a law enforcement academy) will understand the complex nuances in the laws of "Search and Seizure." The diagrams and illustrations will aid the student in understanding legal issues that are related to police work. Additionally, the summarized cases explain legal issues in an easy to understand format.

About the Author

Flavio Mota ("Mota") is a Chicago Police Officer. Mota taught law (Driving Under the Influence, Search and Seizure--The Fourth Amendment, Crimes Against Property, Crimes Against People, Rules of Admission, and other subjects), for over three years, at The Chicago Police Academy. Additionally, Mota teaches the aforementioned subjects at the university level. Mota has a Bachelor's degree (in Criminal Science) with Honors and High distinction from The University of Illinois at Chicago. Additionally, Mota graduated from Chicago Kent College of Law with two law degrees (J.D. and LL.M., an advanced law degree). Mota is a member of the Illinois Bar. (Mota is licensed to practice law in Illinois.)

Chapter 1

History of the Fourth Amendment

Objective:

1. The student will be able to define the Exclusionary Rule and its effects on law enforcement functions.

The Fourth Amendment of the United States Constitution controls the majority of the police officers' search and seizure actions. Before the Fourth Amendment was enacted, the King of England had the power to order people to search, without any evidence of wrongdoing—just because the king felt like it, the homes of people. Through "writs of assistance," also called general warrants, the king had the power to search the houses of people. (This power was used to enforce the revenue laws—to make sure that people were paying the taxes that they were supposed to.) [1]

Along with enforcing the revenue laws, the power to search the homes of people was used to harass people by invading their privacy and rummaging through their homes. The Fourth Amendment to the United States Constitution was enacted to limit the government's power to conduct searches without any evidence:[2]

> The right of the people to be secure in their persons, houses, papers, and effects, against unreasonable searches and seizures, shall not be violated, and no Warrants shall issue, but upon probable cause, supported by Oath or affirmation, and particularly describing the place to be searched, and the persons or things to be seized.[3]

---

[1] James Otis, *Against Writs of Assistance*, (1761) (This writing provides a good history of searches prior to the Fourth Amendment.).

[2] *Id.*

[3] U.S. Const. amend. IV.

Technically, the Fourth Amendment regulates only the "search and seizure" actions of the Federal Government.[4]

For practical purposes, the Fourth Amendment applies to all governmental police officers. (This means that the Fourth Amendment restricts the police powers of federal, state, and local police officers.)[5] **The important thing for any governmental police officer to understand is that the Fourth Amendment applies to him or her. Put another way, all police officers are governed by the Fourth Amendment.**

The Supreme Court of the United States

Related to the Constitution of the United States ("the Constitution"), the Supreme Court of the United States ("the Supreme Court"), the highest court in the country, interprets the Constitution.[6] Additionally, the Supreme Court decides constitutional questions; and its decisions are binding on the lower courts.[7] **In other words, all the lower courts have to obey the rulings of the Supreme Court.[8] The decisions of the Supreme Court become the law of the land.[9]**

Because the states have the authority to provide the citizens with more protection than the Constitution provides, police officers need to be familiar with the search and seizure laws of their states. The Supreme Court sets the minimum standards of protection against governmental interference. The states have the authority to provide more protection; but the states cannot provide less protection than the decisions of the Supreme Court. (Instructors, who are using this book for training, must be well versed with the search and seizure laws of their states.

[4] The first ten amendments to the Constitution of the United States apply to the federal government only.

[5] *Mapp v. Ohio*, 367 U.S. 643 (1961) (The Supreme Court ruled that state and local governments, through the Fourteenth Amendment, are restricted by the Fourth Amendment.).

[6] *Marbury v. Madison*, 5 U.S. (1 Cranch) 137 (1803) (This is an interesting case because the Supreme Court, while deciding an issue that was completely unrelated to the Supreme Court's authority over the Constitution, made it very clear that the Supreme Court was the branch of government responsible for interpreting the Constitution and ruling on constitutional questions.).

[7] *Id.*

[8] So, even though the Congress is responsible for law making, the Supreme Court, by deciding cases and establishing precedents, engages in law making. (When the Supreme Court decides a case, it becomes the law of the land; see the Supremacy clause of the Constitution.).

[9] *Id.*

This book, however, provides a valuable training resource; most of the laws discussed in this book are relevant to all governmental police agencies.)[10]

The Supreme Court held that evidence obtained in violation of the Fourth Amendment might be excluded from trial.[11] **This decision is known as the Exclusionary Rule. (This rule is a possible test question on the Illinois State exam.)[12] So, a police officer might lose his or her case because valuable evidence that is obtained in violation of the Fourth Amendment might not be admissible at the trial. In other words, the Exclusionary Rule prevents the evidence that is seized in violation of the Fourth Amendment from being used in court.** (So, the officer might lose his or her case—the criminal might beat the case. With this in mind, the officer should not violate the Fourth Amendment.)

The Supreme Court, the Fourth Amendment, and the Police Officer

A police officer is responsible for many things; and this book focuses mainly on the "search and seizure" activities of a police officer. Now, with that being said, a police officer drives through the streets with the purpose of preventing crime, detecting crime, apprehending criminals, enforcing the laws, responding to calls for service, and building community relations.[13] Related to these activities, the judges of the Supreme Court, through deciding cases and interpreting the Fourth Amendment, **write the rules that police officers have to follow while they are performing their duties.[14]**

---

[10] The search and seizure laws of a few states provide the citizens more protection. These differences in the law are important because a police officer might lose his or her case. For example, the judge might not allow the use of evidence that was obtained in violation of the state's search and seizure laws.

[11] *Weeks v. United States,* 232 U.S. 383 (1914) (The Supreme Court ruled that the evidence, obtained in violation of the search warrant requirement of the Fourth Amendment, was inadmissible.).

[12] Police recruits in the state of Illinois are required to study this rule because it might be tested on the mandatory state exam.

[13] Community Policing is an important aspect of patrol—police officers interact with the public to build relationships, get citizens to cooperate with the police, and get information. While Community Policing is a crucial aspect of a police officer's job, it is beyond the scope of this book. Additionally, police officers, besides driving in a car, perform their duties while walking, riding bicycles, on motorcycles, on boats, and so on; but this is not an introductory book on policing.

[14] There are consequences for an officer who does not follow the rules; the consequences can include recovered evidence being held inadmissible, a departmental reprimand, a lawsuit (an officer, under Section 1983, can be personally sued—in other words, the officer has to pay out of his or her pocket), and separation from the job.

A police officer must follow these rules, when he or she is dealing with people or private property. Related to a police officer's encounters with people, there are four types of police interactions with the public:

1. consensual encounters—these encounters do not implicate the Fourth Amendment and require no police justification,[15]

2. caretaker encounters—the Supreme Court has acknowledged that these types of encounters are legitimate police/citizen encounters,[16]

3. investigatory seizures—these encounters require justification (the person or persons are not free to leave and the encounter is not a consensual one, reasonable suspicion is needed), also known as *Terry* stops (after the big case that created them),[17] and

4. arrests—these are encounters of the highest level (probable cause is needed), the person or persons are not free to leave and they are going to jail.

It is extremely important that students become familiar with the different levels of encounters. By being familiar with these encounters, a police officer will be able to do police work without violating the Fourth Amendment. Simply put, an officer will be able to do excellent police work without violating people's rights. In the following chapters, these levels of encounters are discussed in great detail.

Related to police/citizen encounters, a police officer needs to be aware of the different levels of evidence that are required for searches. **The evidence that is required for a police/citizen encounter is separate from the evidence that is required for a search.** Put another way, in most situations, a police officer needs

---

[15] *Royer v. Florida,* 460 U.S. 491 (1983) (The Supreme Court held that a police officer can walk up to any person on the street and have a conversation without the encounter being a seizure; a consensual encounter does not involve the Fourth Amendment.).

[16] *Cady v. Dombrowski,* 413 U.S. (1973).

[17] *Terry v. Ohio,* 392 U.S. 1 (1968)(The Supreme Court ruled that a police officer, based on reasonable articulable suspicion of a crime—about to be committed, in progress, or just committed—is allowed to forcibly detain a subject; this type of seizure does not amount to an arrest.).

to justify (1) the reason for the police/citizen encounter and (2) the reason for the search. Moreover, there are different levels of justification for police searches:

1. "plain view"—there is no Fourth Amendment implication,[18]

2. "community caretaker search"—the police officer's main concern is the safety of others,[19]

3. "protective frisks"—reasonable suspicion that the person is "armed and dangerous" is required,[20] and

4. search warrants—probable cause is required for this type of searches.

Other types of searches are discussed in the following chapters. **The student should realize that the above-mentioned proof levels, for searches, are very similar to the levels of proof that are required for the different types of police/citizen encounters. Understanding this is important because it will make the overall understanding of search and seizure a lot easier.**

---

[18] *Horton v. California,* 496 U.S. 128 (1990) (The "plain view" doctrine does not violate the Fourth Amendment.).
[19] Cady, 413 U.S.
[20] *Terry,* 392 U.S. 1.

Review

Objective:

1. Define the Exclusionary Rule and identify its effect on the law enforcement function.

- The Supreme Court held that evidence obtained in violation of the Fourth Amendment might be excluded from trial.[21] **This decision is known as the Exclusionary Rule. (This rule is a possible test question on the Illinois State exam.)**[22] **Therefore, a police officer might lose his or her case because valuable evidence obtained in violation of the Fourth Amendment might not be admissible at the trial. In other words, the Exclusionary Rule prevents the evidence that is seized in violation of the Fourth Amendment from being used in court. (So, the officer might lose his or her case—the criminal might beat the case.** With this in mind, the officer should not violate the Fourth Amendment.)

Conclusion

In summary, this has been a very brief overview of the Fourth Amendment, search and seizure law, policing, and required levels of proof. The following chapters, however, provide more explanations and cases. Additionally, illustrations, examples, summaries of major cases, and student exercises are included in the following chapters. Good luck to you.

[21] Weeks v. United States, 232 U.S. 383 (1914).

[22] Police recruits in the state of Illinois are required to study this rule because it might be tested on the mandatory state exam.

Review Questions

1. What amount of evidence is needed for a police officer to have a consensual encounter on the public way?

2. What amount of evidence is needed for a police officer to seize a person?

3. What amount of evidence is needed for a police officer to arrest a person?

4. Describe the exclusionary rule.

5. How does the Fourth Amendment affect citizens?

6. How does the Fourth Amendment affect police officers?

Notes

Date:

Notes

Date:

Chapter 2

The Police Officer on Patrol

Objectives:

The student will be able to

1. define probable cause,
2. define reasonable suspicion,
3. define arrest warrant, and
4. define frisk.

Police officers have numerous encounters with the public. Some of these encounters are consensual. (These types of encounters do not implicate the Fourth Amendment and a police officer does not have to legally justify the consensual encounters.) Other encounters, where the subject is forcefully detain, do require legal justification. Put another way, if the subject is not free to leave, then a legal justification for the seizure is required. Forceful detentions, however, are allowed.[23]

The Supreme Court has recognized four types of encounters:

1. the consensual encounter,
2. the caretaker encounter,
3. the investigatory seizure (also known as the *Terry* stop), and
4. the full-blown custodial arrest.

For the consensual encounter, the police officer does not need a legal justification. In other words, suspicion, proof, of criminal activity is not required. This means that a police officer may legally approach anyone on the public way and start a conversation with that person. During a consensual encounter, however, the subject is free to walk away.[24] With **reasonable suspicion**, a police officer can legally seize (forcefully detain) a person for the purpose of conducting an investigation.[25] This type of encounter is not a custodial arrest; this means that the *Miranda* warnings are not required. (The *Miranda* warnings will be discussed later.)

---

[23] *Terry, 392 U.S. 1.*
[24] *Royer,* 460 U.S.
[25] *Terry,* 392 U.S. 1.

Diagram 2.1

THE LEVELS OF POLICE ENCOUNTERS

THE CUSTODIAL ARREST

- NEED PROBABLE CAUSE TO BELIEVE THAT A CRIME WAS COMMITTED AND THAT THE PERSON ARRESTED COMMITTED THE CRIME

THE *TERRY* STOP
(THE INVESTIGATORY SEIZURE)

- NEED REASONABLE SUSPICION FOR (1) THE SEIZURE AND (2) THE FRISK
- IT IS A TWO PART TEST

THE CARETAKER ENCOUNTER

- A PERSON'S WELFARE IS A CONCERN
- THE PROTECTION OF PROPERTY IS A CONCERN

THE CONSENSUAL ENCOUNTER

- NO SUSPICION OF CRIMINAL ACTIVITY IS NEEDED
- THE PERSON IS FREE TO GO
- THE PERSON HAS THE RIGHT TO DENY CONSENT

The Consensual Encounter

The Supreme Court has ruled that police officers can approach people who are on the public way and ask questions. As long as the reasonable person would feel free to walk away, a seizure has not occurred. Additionally, police officers, during a consensual encounter, can ask for consent to search the property of the person(s) whom the police officers are talking with. During this consensual encounter, the person is free to refuse to talk to the police and to walk away. In addition, the person's refusal to talk or walking away does not give the police officer authority to seize the person. These actions do not amount to reasonable suspicion of criminal activity.

For example, a police officer can approach a person on the street and ask for consent to search his or her person. As long as the officer is being polite (not making any threats) and the encounter is consensual, the officer can arrest the person if the search reveals something that is illegal.[26] There are factors that will turn a consensual encounter into a seizure. For example, if the officer

1. orders the person to stop,
2. grabs the person,
3. has a weapon in hand when dealing with the person, or
4. handcuffs the person,

then the encounter is a seizure; a seizure requires reasonable suspicion. (There are many factors that can make the encounter a seizure; some of the factors are called *Mendenhall* factors and will be discussed later.)

The Caretaker Encounter

The Supreme Court created the caretaker encounter. A police officer who is primarily concerned with the welfare of a person or property is legally allowed to investigate the situation or to interfere with property. For example, a police officer who observes an unconscious person in a legally parked car is allowed to tap on the car window, open the car door, or shake the person to make sure that the person is all right. In addition, a police officer is allowed to take control of property for the protection of the property. This type of encounter requires an explanation from the officer.

---

[26] *Florida v. Bostick*, 501 U.S. 429 (1991) (The Supreme Court held that police officers are allowed to approach people who are on public places and ask for consent to search their persons; as long as the reasonable person would feel free to say no, the encounter is consensual; and the consent to search—if given—is valid.).

Terry v. Ohio (1968)

In *Terry v. Ohio*, Officer McFadden, a police detective with 39 years of experience observed two men on Huron Road. One man would stand on a corner while the other man would walk to a store window and look inside the store. After the man looked inside the store, he would walk away from the store and confer with the man on the corner. The two men took turns walking to the store and looking inside the store. They repeated this pattern about twelve times. Thereafter, a third man joined the two men.

After about twelve minutes, after McFadden had become suspicious; he suspected that the three men were casing the store. In other words, he suspected that they were about to commit a robbery.

Officer McFadden considered it his duty to investigate the three men. So, he approached the three men and asked for their names. In response to his inquiries, one of the men mumbled something. At this point Officer McFadden grabbed Terry and spun him around so that he was facing the other two men. Officer McFadden patted down Terry's outer clothing and felt a pistol on the left pocket of Terry's coat. Officer McFadden ordered the three men to go inside Zucker's store. Inside the store, McFadden removed Terry's coat and ordered the three men to face a wall and to raise their hands. Officer McFadden recovered .38 caliber revolver from Terry's coat. Additionally, Officer McFadden recovered a second revolver form Chilton's coat. Subsequently, Officer McFadden asked the owner of the store to call the police and request a wagon. And Officer McFadden took the three men to the police station. Chilton and Terry were charged with carrying concealed weapons.

Chilton and Terry were found guilty of carrying concealed weapons. The Supreme Court of the United States ("the Supreme Court") granted certiorari. In other words, The Supreme Court agreed to review whether the admission of the firearms as evidence was constitutional. This was crucial because if the weapons were excluded from evidence, the conviction had to be overturned. Put another way, Terry's conviction could not stand and he would be a free man. (Before the Supreme Court reviewed the case, Chilton died. So, the Supreme Court only reviewed Terry's case.)

The question before the Supreme Court was whether Officer McFadden violated Terry's Fourth Amendment right (made applicable to the states through the Fourteenth Amendment under *Mapp v. Ohio*) to be free from unreasonable searches and seizures. The Supreme Court acknowledged that the detention of a citizen by the police is more than a petty indignity. At the same time, the Supreme Court acknowledged that the police need some power in order to effectively perform their jobs (prevent crime).

In resolving this issue, the Supreme Court stated that Terry's detention did implicate the Fourth Amendment. The court concluded that Terry's detention was a seizure and that it was a reasonable one. The court considered Officer McFadden's experience in deciding the reasonableness of the seizure.

In conclusion, related to seizures, Terry v. Ohio is significant because it allows police officers to detain citizens, perform protective pat-downs (a limited search for weapons), and ask questions on less than probable cause. The police officer needs to have reasonable suspicion that criminal activity is "afoot." (In other words the officer needs reasonable suspicion that criminal activity is about to occur, is occurring, or has just occurred.) Simply put, an explanation is needed.

Overview of Reasonable Suspicion

In 1968, the Supreme Court ruled that a police officer is allowed to forcefully detain a subject for the purpose of conducting an investigation. The Supreme Court stated that an officer who has **reasonable articulable suspicion of criminal activity** can lawfully detain a subject against his or her will.[27] This type of temporary detention is not a custodial arrest. Another name for this type of encounter is the *Terry* stop. It is known as the *Terry* stop because of the Supreme Court case *Terry v. Ohio*.[28]

In *Terry v. Ohio*, a veteran detective observed three males casing (planning to rob) a store. Detective McFadden physically grabbed one of the males and performed a **frisk.** A frisk is a limited search for weapons. And Detective McFadden found a firearm on the male. Consequently, the male was arrested because of the pistol. Detective McFadden did two things that implicated the Fourth Amendment.

1. Detective McFadden seized the male.
2. Detective McFadden searched the male.

At the time, when Detective McFadden grabbed and seized the male subject, holding a person against his or her will amounted to a custodial arrest. Put another way, Detective McFadden needed **probable cause** to detain and search the subject. And Detective McFadden did not have enough facts to articulate **probable cause.**

Even though Detective McFadden did not have **probable cause,** the Supreme Court stated that the seizure and search of the male subject were reasonable. Stated differently, the Supreme Court created a new law that allows police officers to physically detain and perform limited searches (for weapons only) based on **reasonable suspicion.** Based on this, it follows that **reasonable suspicion** is a lower standard than **probable cause.** (For more information on *Terry v. Ohio*, please read the summary of the case.)

---

[27] *Terry*, 392 U.S. 1.
[28] *Id.*

The *Terry v. Ohio* case is important to police officers because it allows police officers to physically detain people for the purpose of conducting investigations. Officers are allowed to perform investigatory stops, based on **reasonable suspicion of criminal activity,** without placing people under custodial arrests, which require **probable cause**.

The Meaning of Reasonable Suspicion

Reasonable suspicion is the level of proof that is required for an investigatory seizure and a frisk for weapons. The standard is higher than a mere hunch or bare suspicion. And it is a lower standard than probable cause.[29] It is important for officers to be aware that a search and a frisk require two separate tests.

Again, a frisk is a limited search for weapons only. The search is allowed to protect officers and the public from a potentially dangerous person who has been seized. It is not a search for drugs or other non-weapon contraband. The officer is allowed to frisk (pat-down) the person whom the officer is dealing with based on reasonable articulable suspicion that the person is presently armed and dangerous. During the frisk, if the officer feels something that might be a weapon (for example, feels a firearm, knife, or hard object that might be a weapon), then the officer is allowed to retrieve the item from the subject's person. Going immediately into the pockets (without first feeling an item that might be a weapon) is not allowed. (There is a plain touch law that allows officers to retrieve narcotics from the person; this will be discussed later.)

So, for the investigatory detention, the officer has to be able to say why the subject was detained. An explanation saying that the subject or the situation looked suspicious is not enough. This is not reasonable articulable suspicion. This is called bare suspicion. Again, bare suspicion is not enough for an investigatory detention.[30] And the officer has to articulate why the (1) seizure and (2) the frisk were performed. (In situations where a frisk is not made, the officer only has to explain why the seizure was made. Only one justification is required.)

---

[29] *Id.*

[30] *Brown v. Texas*, 443 U.S. 47 (1979) (The arresting officer testified, in court, that he conducted an investigatory detention because the situation "looked suspicious…." And the Supreme Court said that bare suspicion is not enough for an investigatory detention. In other words some articulation of why the situation is suspicious is required.).

Diagram 2.2

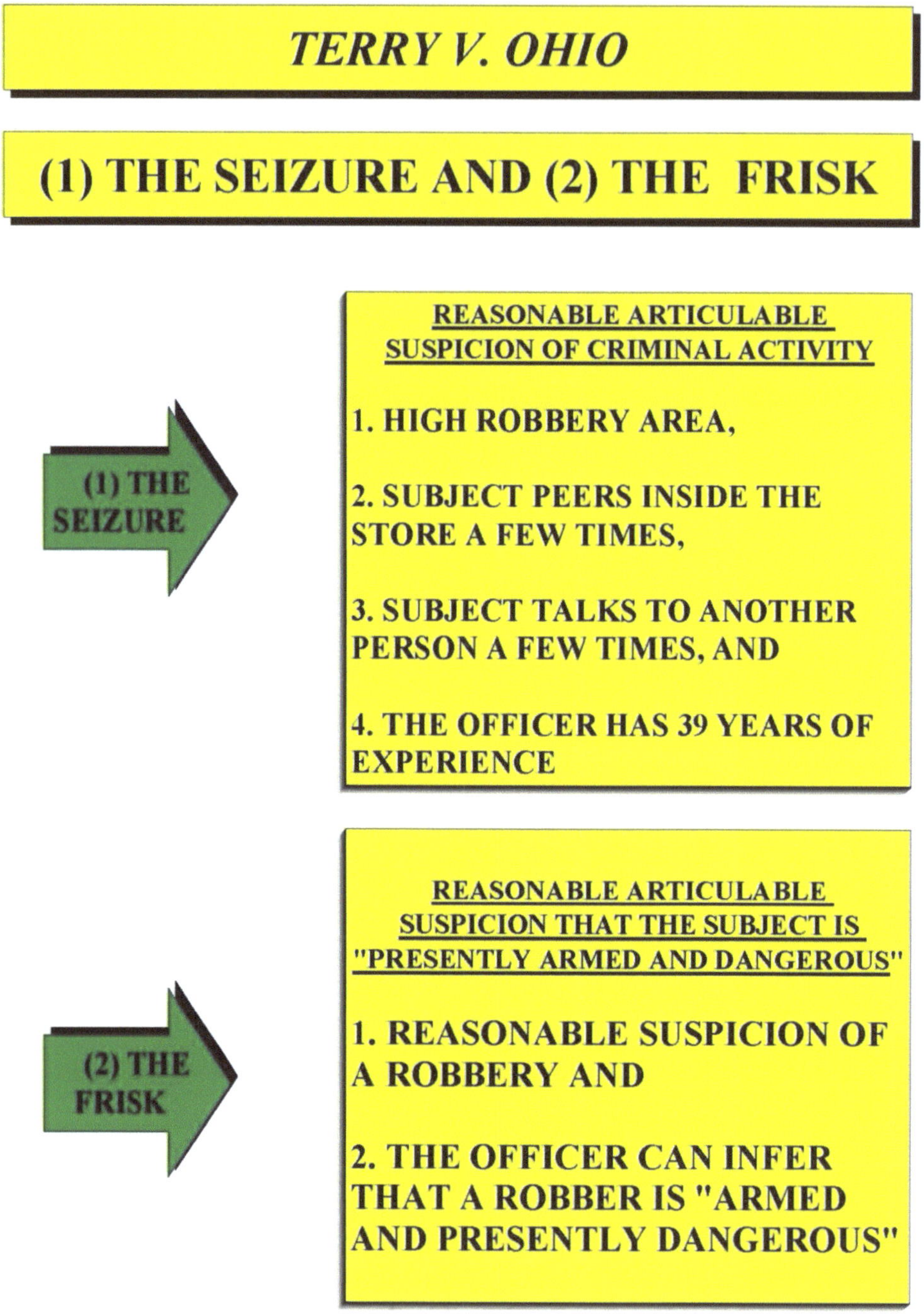

TERRY V. OHIO
(1) THE SEIZURE AND (2) THE FRISK
(1) THE SEIZURE
REASONABLE ARTICULABLE SUSPICION OF CRIMINAL ACTIVITY
1. HIGH ROBBERY AREA,
2. SUBJECT PEERS INSIDE THE STORE A FEW TIMES,
3. SUBJECT TALKS TO ANOTHER PERSON A FEW TIMES, AND
4. THE OFFICER HAS 39 YEARS OF EXPERIENCE
(2) THE FRISK
REASONABLE ARTICULABLE SUSPICION THAT THE SUBJECT IS "PRESENTLY ARMED AND DANGEROUS"
1. REASONABLE SUSPICION OF A ROBBERY AND
2. THE OFFICER CAN INFER THAT A ROBBER IS "ARMED AND PRESENTLY DANGEROUS"

In the first test, the officer is required to explain why the subject or the situation is suspicious. For example, in *Terry*, the officer stated that one of the subjects looked into the store a few times, paced back and forth, talked to another person. Also, the officer stated that, based on these facts, he suspected that the subjects where casing the store for a robbery. The officer articulated why the situation looked suspicious. The officer articulated a few facts to support why the situation looked suspicious. And the court ruled that the investigatory stop was legal.[31]

Many times, an officer will perform a frisk for weapons. The frisk requires a separate explanation from the seizure. In situations in which a seizure and a frisk are performed, the second part of the test is whether the officer can articulate reasonable suspicion that led him or her to believe that the seized person was armed and presently dangerous. To be clear, the officer has to explain why (1) the seizure was made and (2) why a frisk was performed.

It is important that police officers understand that saying that the frisk was performed "for officer safety" is not enough to legally justify the frisk. [32] (Protective frisks are extremely important for officer safety.) Police officers are required to give a reason.

> **Example 2.1: The arresting officer observed the vehicle drive through a solid red light. The arresting officer ordered the driver of the car to pull over. After the car came to a stop, the driver (1) jumped out of the car and started (2) screaming "why are you stopping me!" The driver (3) did not comply with the officer's order to get back in the car. Additionally, (4) the driver was nervous (visibly shaking). For these reasons, the arresting officer believed that the driver was armed and dangerous. So, the arresting officer performed a protective frisk; and the protective frisk revealed an illegal blue steel .38 caliber revolver.**

[31] It is not enough for the police officer to say that the situation looked suspicious. The police officer has to say what factors led him or her to believe that the situation looked suspicious. The police officer should articulate as many factors as were present.

[32] The author understands that protective frisks are important for officer safety; and the author is not against protective frisks. But the officer is going to discuss how officers can legally perform and legally explain protective frisks.

Example 2.2: After stopping a car for expired plates, (1) the police officer observed a bulge in the driver's waist. And (2) the driver was verbally combative, cursing. Additionally, the (3) driver was nervous—shaking. Consequently, the officer performed a frisk and recovered an illegal pistol, a .45 automatic.

Example 2.3: (1) In a high robbery area, (2) A face-to-face complainant (who was very credible—tone of voice, eye contact, spoke with confidence) told the police officer that the person, who is sitting in the white Chevrolet Monte Carlo across the street, has a firearm in his waistband. Consequently, the officer approached the person, who was in the Monte Carlo, and recovered an illegal automatic firearm (.40 mm) from the subject's waistband. (In this example, the statement of the credible citizen is enough to justify (1) the seizure and (2) the frisk.)[33]

In the above examples, the officers explained—in the highlighted portion—why the frisk was performed. In the first example, the officer gave four (4) factors (or reasons) for the frisk. How many factors are needed? The Supreme Court has not answered that question. A judge is more likely to rule that the frisk was justified if the police officer gives three (3) or more factors; and a judge will probably rule that one (1) factor is not enough. This means that the police officer should give as many factors as were present during the *Terry* stop, the seizure. (During the seizure, the police officer has to be aware of his or her surroundings and be alert; this way the police officer can explain all the factors that occurred during the seizure.)

During the seizure and frisk, if the officer uncovers an illegal weapon (for example, an illegal firearm), then the officer has **probable cause** to arrest the person. **Probable cause is the (1) level of evidence that is required by the Fourth Amendment to make a custodial arrest and the (2) level of required evidence to perform a search.** (A search is different from a frisk because a search is more intrusive than a frisk.)[34]

---

[33] See *Adams v. Williams,* 407 U.S. 143 (1972) (The Supreme Court ruled that a face-to-face conversation with a third party who stated that the subject was carrying a firearm and drugs is a strong factor that can be used, in conjunction with other factors, to justify both a stop and a frisk.).

[34] A "frisk" is a "search," but it is a limited search. Therefore, even though, a frisk and a "search" are both searches, it is important for students to understand the difference between the two.

Additionally, during the seizure, the police officer can check to see if there is an arrest warrant for the subject. **A warrant is an order from a judge (a neutral magistrate) for the arrest of a person. Illinois (in 725 ILCS 5/107-1) defines arrest warrant as an order from a court that directs a peace officer to arrest a person;**

> **[a] "warrant of arrest" is a written order from a court directed to a peace officer, or some other person specifically named, commanding him to arrest a person.**

A judge has the power to issue a warrant when a person does not show up to a scheduled court hearing. Additionally, a judge, after being presented with probable cause of a crime, has the authority to approve an arrest warrant for the arrest of the person suspected of committing the crime.

The Meaning of Probable Cause

As mentioned before, and related to arrests, probable cause is the amount of evidence that is required by the Fourth Amendment for a lawful arrest. It is similar to **reasonable suspicion** because it works the same way. The difference is that probable cause is a higher standard of proof. This means that a police officer needs more evidence than is required for a seizure. Put simply, the police officer has to articulate why the arrest was made.

The test of whether or not probable cause exists is a non-technical analysis, according to the Supreme Court; based on the totality of the circumstances, is there enough information for an objectively reasonable police officer to conclude that the person to be arrested committed a crime? (Or, for a search warrant, is there enough evidence for the reasonable and objective police officer to conclude that something illegal will be found in the place to be searched?)[35] In explaining the probable cause for the incident, the

[35] *Brinegar v. United States,* 338 U.S. 160, 175 (1949) (The Supreme Court stated that probable cause is a practical and non-technical concept; reasonable inferences are allowed from facts and observations. Practical considerations of everyday life are applied.); *Carrol v. United States,* 267 U.S. 132, 162 (1925) (The Supreme Court said that probable cause exists if the facts and circumstances "warrant a man of reasonable caution" in the strong belief that a crime has been committed.); *Illinois v. Gates,* 426 U.S. 213, 230 (1982) (The Supreme Court stated that

police officer is allowed to make inferences, make conclusions from his or her experience, and to use his or her training. (Please note, older cases, older textbooks, outdated training, and older legal sources use the reasonable and prudent person standard. The correct standard is the "objectively reasonable police officer" standard.)[36] To repeat, for a lawful arrest—supported by probable cause, some evidence is needed. The officer does not need enough evidence to get a conviction.[37] But the officer does need more evidence than a mere hunch or unarticulated suspicion.[38]

Additionally, the Supreme Court has stated that a police officer's mere subjective belief that he or she was doing the right thing by arresting the person does not amount to probable cause.[39] (This means that the police officer has to explain why the arrest was made or why a search was conducted without getting a warrant; the situations when an officer is allowed to search without a warrant will be discussed later.)

"the totality of the circumstances" approach is the test to use to determine if probable cause exists; this means that everything that is available is considered. Additionally, the court, citing *Brinegar,* stressed that probable cause deals with probabilities; this means that the more information that the officer gives the more likely that probable cause exists.); *Ornelas v. United States,* 517 U.S. 690, (1996) (The Supreme Court stated that "the objectively reasonable police officer" test is the one to use when determining whether probable cause exists.).

[36] *Ornelas,* 517 U.S. 690 (The Supreme Court stated that the layperson does not have the training and experience to detect criminal activity at the level that a police officer is able to.).

[37] The standard for a conviction is "beyond a reasonable doubt." A police officer does not need to prove that the person is guilty "beyond a reasonable doubt." But the police officer does need to prove probable cause which is a substantially lower standard than "beyond a reasonable doubt." Probable cause is a higher standard than "reasonable suspicion." To repeat, the police officer has to show and explain some facts that support probable cause for the arrest (or search). *Brinegar,* 338 U.S. 160.

[38] A mere hunch or an unarticulated suspicion will not justify a seizure. So, a mere hunch or an unarticulated suspicion will definitely not justify an arrest. (Reasonable suspicion is needed for a seizure.) Probable cause lies between the reasonable suspicion standard and the proof beyond a reasonable doubt standard.

[39] *Beck v. Ohio,* 379 U.S. 89, 97 (1964) (The Supreme Court (Citing *Henry v. United States,* 361 U.S. 98 (1959) stated that an officer's belief that he or she is acting in good faith is not enough for probable cause.). To elaborate further, if an arrest that is made without probable cause reveals something illegal—for example, and illegal firearm—the illegal item will not justify the arrest. This means that probable cause is needed before the arrest is made.

Scenario 2.1

While patrolling a high crime neighborhood (it is known for thefts, shoplifting, and robberies), Officer Jones observes a male subject standing by a jewelry store. Officer Jones has been a police officer for over thirty years. Additionally, Officer Jones is assigned to investigate robberies in the area. Consequently, Officer Jones, unseen by the male subject by the jewelry store, positions himself where he can observe the male subject.

Officer Jones witnesses the male subject peek four times through the store's glass windows. Also, the male subject walked to the corner three times to converse with another male. Additionally both subjects are wearing heavy coats; the temperature is eighty degrees. This is suspicious to Officer Jones; the situation does not look right. **(Officer Jones considers it his duty to perform an investigation).** So, Officer Jones calls for backup and Officer Smith arrives along with several other officers.

The Officers push the two male subjects against the wall and perform **frisks** on both subjects. The subjects are physically detained and they are not free to walk away. The **frisks** reveal two loaded sawed-off shotguns—one on each subject. Because it is against the law to carry a loaded sawed-off shotgun, the officers have **probable cause** to arrest both subjects. Consequently, the subjects are arrested and transported to the police station.

At the station, background checks reveal that both of the arrestees have **arrest warrants** for failure to show up to court on previous criminal charges.

Discussion Questions

1. Did the officers have the legal authority under the Fourth Amendment to detain the subjects?
2. Did the officers have the legal authority under the Fourth Amendment to frisk—search—the subjects?
3. At what point were the subjects arrested?
4. How would you articulate your **reasonable suspicion** and **probable cause** on the arrest paperwork?

Review

<u>Objectives</u>:

1. Define probable cause.

- Probable cause is the amount of evidence that would give the objectively reasonable police officer a strong belief that a crime was committed and that the person to be arrested committed the offence.[40] (Be aware that the old law is still sometimes used; probable cause is information that would give the reasonable and prudent person a strong belief that a crime was committed and that the person to be arrested committed the offense.)[41]

2. Define reasonable suspicion.

- Reasonable suspicion is the level of proof that is required for an investigatory seizure and a frisk for weapons. The standard is higher than a mere hunch or bare suspicion. And it is a lower standard than probable cause. It is important for officers to be aware that a stop and a frisk require two separate tests.[42]

3. Define arrest warrant.

- [a] "warrant of arrest" is a written order from a court directed to a peace officer, or some other person specifically named, commanding him to arrest a person.[43]

---

[40] *Ornelas,* 517 U.S. 690.
[41] *Brinegar,* 338 U.S. 160.
[42] *Terry,* 392 U.S. 1.
[43] See 725 ILCS 5/107-1. This is Illinois's definition of arrest warrant.

4. Define frisk.

- A frisk is a limited search for weapons only. The search is allowed to protect officers and the public from a potentially dangerous person who has been seized. It is not a search for drugs or other non-weapon contraband. The officer is allowed to frisk (pat-down) the person whom the officer is dealing with based on reasonable articulable suspicion that the person is presently armed and dangerous. During the frisk, if the officer feels something that might be a weapon (for example, feels a firearm, knife, or hard object that might be a weapon), then the officer is allowed to retrieve the item from the subject's person. Going immediately into the pockets (without first feeling an item that might be a weapon) is not allowed.[44] (There is a plain touch law that allows officers to retrieve narcotics from the person; this will be discussed later.)

Conclusion

The following chapters contain more examples and explanations. One of the things to remember is that, when a police officer seizes and frisks a person, two explanations are required: one for the seizure one for the frisk. The levels of police encounters were discussed in this chapter. Also, related to police work, the police officer should be able to articulate facts that led to the officer's decisions and actions.

[44] *Terry*, 392 U.S. 1.

Review Questions

1. What is a frisk?

2. What does reasonable suspicion mean?

3. What is an arrest warrant?

4. What is a stop (seizure)?

5. Describe the importance of *Terry v. Ohio*.

6. How many explanations are required when a police officer seizes and frisks a person?

7. List all the police/citizen encounters that the Supreme Court has recognized.

___

___

___

8. Describe the "care taker role" encounter.

___

___

___

9. Describe a situation when a police officer will have reasonable suspicion to believe that a person is "presently armed and dangerous."

___

___

___

10. Describe three situations when a police officer has probable cause to arrest people.

___

___

___

___

11. What does a police officer need for a valid consensual search? ___

___

Notes

Date:

Notes

Date:

Notes

Date:

Notes

Date:

Chapter 3
Notices to Appear

Objectives:

The student will be able to
1. define notice to appear,
2. recognize circumstances when the issuance of a notice to appear is authorized in non-traffic cases,
3. identify the proper procedures for the issuance of a notice to appear in non-traffic cases, and
4. identify the requisites of a notice to appear.

Notices to Appear

While on patrol, a police officer will have many encounters with citizens. Additionally, a police officer will observe suspicious activity. Additionally, the police officer will observe criminal activity or ordinance violations. **Sometimes, during these events, the police officer will discover a violation of a city ordinance or a minor criminal offense for which the police officer has the option of issuing a notice to appear.**

A notice to appear is a document issued by a police officer to a person requesting the person to appear in court. Illinois's definition (725 ILCS 5/107-1) of "a notice to appear is as follows:

> **[a] "notice to appear" is written request issued by a peace officer that a person appear before a court at a stated time and place.**[45]

Most people know "a notice to appear" as a ticket. A notice to appear is a ticket. It is a ticket that requires the violator (of a minor crime or an ordinance violation) to appear in court. (Sometimes the violator will have the option of paying a fine and not going to court.) The situations when a police officer may issue "a notice to appear" are state or city specific.

---

[45] See 725 ILCS 5/107-1(c). The statute gives the source of the definition: Laws 1963, p. 2836. The author added the emphasis—the boldface.

For example, in Chicago (Illinois), there are many situations for when a police officer may issue "a notice to appear." Keep in mind that the examples are for Chicago. These tickets might not be available in other police departments.

<u>Chicago examples</u>:

1. 8-4-030	Drinking alcohol on the public way
2. 9-80-200(b)	Skateboarding in business district
3. 10-8-310	Placing advertising materials on automobiles
4. 10-8-410	Skating on public street
5. 10-8-520	Unlicensed vendor on public way or in traffic lane
6. 10-36-130	Glass in park, playground, beach
7. 10-36-185***	Alcohol on park district property
8. 10-36-185***	Unleashed animal in park
9. 10-36-185***	After hours-[on] Park District property
10. 7-24-099	Possession of cannabis (15 grams or less)

When a police officer issues a "notice to appear," the ticket takes the place of a full-blown custodial arrest. Put another way, the infractions are arrestable offenses. When the officer issues a ticket, instead of making a custodial arrest, the officer saves time because the custodial arrest is more time consuming than the writing of the ticket. This allows the officer more time to patrol instead of being inside the station processing the custodial arrest.

Notices to appear are usually issued for minor offenses. And the offenses for which a notice to appear may be given are controlled by state law (a state statute). For example, in Illinois, the statute states that a notice to appear may be issued whenever a police officer is authorized to arrest without a warrant:

> **[w]henever a peace officer is authorized to arrest a person without a warrant he may instead issue to such person a notice to appear.**[46]

Additionally, some police departments put further restrictions on the issuance of notices to appear. For example, a police department might make certain offenses ineligible for a notice to appear. (Prior to 2012, in Chicago, a notice to appear for possessing cannabis, 15 grams or less, was not available. Now, a police officer has the option to issue a notice to appear for possessing cannabis, 15 grams or less.)

[46] See 725 ILCS 5/107-12(a) (citing P.A. 83-693). The boldface was added by the author.

Notice to Appear

Respondent's name (violator) ______________________

Respondent's address ______________________

Respondent's phone number ______________________

Identification type and number ______________________

Respondent's date of birth ______________________

Respondent's height, weight, sex ______________________

Respondent's race and eye color ______________________

Police event number (incident #) ______________________

The ordinance that was violated ______________________

Description of the ordinance ______________________

____

Explain how the ordinance was violated

____

____

Date and time of the violation ______________________

Officer's unit, star #, and signature ______________________

Date, time, location, and room # of the hearing ______________________

____

Respondent's signature (the person ticketed) ______________________

Procedures for the Issuance of a Notice to Appear

Reliable identification from the violator is required. Can the violator be located if he or she fails to show up to court? Also, some police departments require that the police officer check the background of the violator for outstanding warrants. If there is a valid and serviceable warrant, then the police officer must arrest the violator. (An arrest warrant is an order from a court commanding—ordering—a police officer to arrest the person who is named in the arrest warrant.) Additionally, some departments require an incident number for the notice to appear. (This just means that the officer has to obtain a number from dispatch for the encounter with the violator.) Furthermore, the police officer has to sign the notice to appear. (By doing so, the police officer is attesting that the incident—violation—did occur.) So, here is an example of the procedures that might be required of a police officer:

1. reliable identification (Can the subject be located?),
2. a check for arrest warrants,
3. an event number, and
4. a signature from the police officer.

The procedures are different for different police departments. The above mentioned procedures are some of the requirements of the Chicago Police Department. In addition, there are requisites of the notice to appear. Put another way, specific information must be written on the notice to appear.

Requisites of a Notice to Appear

Requisites of a notice to appear are requirements that must be written on the notice to appear. And the requirements vary from police department to police department. And, in some cases, the bare-bones requirements are spelled out in the state statute. **In Illinois, according to 725 ILCS 5/107-12, for example, there are a minimum of five requirements.**

> **(b) The notice shall:**
> **(1) Be in writing;**
> **(2) State the name of the person and his address, if known;**
> **(3) Set forth the nature of the offense;**
> **(4) Be signed by the officer issuing the notice; and**

(5) Request the person to appear before a court at a certain time and place.[47]

To repeat, the notice to appear requisites will vary from state to state and from police department to police department.

Review

Objectives:

1. Define notice to appear.

- "[A] 'notice to appear' is written request issued by a peace officer that a person appear before a court at a stated time and place."[48] Put another way, a notice to appear is a ticket that is issued instead of arresting the law breaker.

2. When is the issuance of a notice to appear (in non-traffic related cases) authorized?

- This will vary from police department to police department. In Illinois, the statute states that a notice to appear may be issued whenever a police officer is authorized to arrest without a warrant:

> [w]henever a peace officer is authorized to arrest a person without a warrant he may instead issue to such person a notice to appear.[49]

[47] See 725 ILCS 5/107-12(b) (citing P.A. 83-693). The boldface was added by the author.
[48] See 725 ILCS 5/107-1(c) (citing Laws 1963, p.2836).
[49] See 725 ILCS 5/107-12(A) (citing P.A. 83-693)

3. What are the proper procedures for the issuance (in non-traffic related cases) of a notice to appear?

- The procedures will vary from police department to police department. But, for the Chicago Police Department, these are a few of the requirements.
  1. reliable identification (Can the subject be located?),
  2. a check for arrest warrants,
  3. an event number, and
  4. a signature from the police officer.

  The state of Illinois stresses the need for reliable identification of the respondent. If the law breaker fails to appear before the court, can the subject be identified and located?

4. What are the requisites of a notice to appear?

- The requisites of a notice to appear will vary from state to state. (And the requisites will be different from police department to police department.) But in Illinois, according to 725 ILCS 5/107-12, the requisites are defined by statute:

  > (b) The notice shall:
  > (1) Be in writing;
  > (2) State the name of the person and his address, if known;
  > (3) Set forth the nature of the offense;
  > (4) Be signed by the officer issuing the notice; and
  > (5) Request the person to appear before a court at a certain time and place.[50]

[50] See 725 ILCS 5/107-12(b) (citing P.A. 83-693).

Conclusion

This was a general overview of the requisites and procedures of the issuance of a notice to appear. And, as discussed before, depending on the police department, there might be additional requirements when issuing a notice to appear. To repeat, a notice to appear is usually given for minor offenses (but arrestable offenses). The student should remember that if the law breaker has an outstanding warrant, then the police officer has no choice but to make the arrest. So, the police officer will make the arrest for the warrant and add the additional offenses to the arrest.

Review Questions

1. What is a notice to appear? ______________________________

____

2. When is a police a police officer authorized to issue a notice to appear? In Illinois, when is a police officer authorized to issue a notice to appear? ______________________________

____

____

____

3. What are the proper procedures for the issuance of a notice to appear? In Illinois, what are the proper procedures for the issuance of a notice to appear? ______________________________

____

____

____

4. What are the requisites of a notice to appear? In Illinois, what are the requisites of a notice to appear? ______________________________

____

____

____

5. What must the police officer do if the law breaker has a valid arrest warrant? ______________________________

____

Notes

Date:

Notes

Date:

Notes

Date:

Notes

Date:

Notes

Date:

Notes

Date:

Chapter 4

Search Warrants, Contraband, Probable Cause, and Arrests

Objectives:

The student will be able to

1. define search warrant,
2. define contraband,
3. identify elements giving rise to probable cause, and
4. recognize circumstances when an arrest without a warrant is authorized.

The Search Warrant

A search warrant is a judge approved order that authorizes the search of a location for specific items. As required by the Fourth Amendment, probable cause is needed for a search warrant. Probable cause is established by "the totality of the circumstances."[51] **According to 725 ILCS 5/108-7, a search warrant is a court issued order:**

> **[t]he warrant shall command the person directed to execute the same to search the place or person particularly described in the warrant and to seize the instruments, articles or things particularly described in the warrant.**[52]

So, to summarize, a search warrant is an order issued by a judge (a neutral magistrate) that authorizes the police to search a particular place for specific items. And it is issued upon a showing of probable cause. (This means that a search warrant is issued upon a showing of a fair probability that something illegal will be found in the place to be searched.) To put the matter another way, based on "the totality of the circumstances," is there a fair probability that a specific illegal item will be found in the place to be searched? If the answer is yes, then there is

[51] *Illinois,* 462 U.S. 213.

[52] See 725 ILCS 5/108-7 (citing Laws 1968, p. 2836). The boldface was added by the author. This is the definition of a search warrant in Illinois. The definitions in other states might vary. But the overall idea is the same; a search warrant is an order from a judge that authorizes the search of a location for specific items.

probable cause for a warrant.[53] (Examples of strong probability, probable cause, will be discussed later.)

Contraband

Contraband is an item that is illegal to possess. For example, a person carrying an illegal firearm (e.g. unregistered). The Supreme Court said that carrying contraband is illegal.[54] Sometimes an item is contraband because the citizen has not met certain criteria. To elaborate, carrying a firearm might be legal in a certain city; but carrying an unregistered pistol might be illegal in that same city. (So, the carrying of the unregistered gun amounts to possessing contraband.) To repeat, contraband is something that is illegal to possess. Many items are contraband; here are a few examples:

1. illegal drugs (for example, marijuana, cocaine, methamphetamine),
2. illegal weapons (for example, assault weapons, sawed-off shotguns),
3. child pornography,
4. counterfeit money, and
5. obscene material for public distribution. (the Supreme Court has not defined what obscene material is; Justice Stewart stated that "I know it when I see it.")[55]

The above list does not have all the things that are contraband. There are many more items that are contraband.

Elements Giving Rise to Probable Cause

According to the Fourth Amendment to the United States, "no warrants shall issue but upon probable cause."[56] Probable cause is the standard of proof that is required by the Fourth Amendment for a Warrant.[57] This means that the police

---

[53] *Illinois v. Gates,* 462 U.S. 213 (1983).

[54] *Illinois v. Caballes,* 543 U.S. 405, 408 (2005) (The Supreme Court said "We have held that any interest in possessing contraband cannot be deemed 'legitimate....'").

[55] *Jacobellis v. Ohio,* 378 U.S. 184 (1964).

[56] U.S. Const. amend. IV.

[57] *Id.*

officer has to explain evidence that amounts to probable cause. Additionally, the police officer is allowed to use "the totality of the circumstances" to prove probable cause.[58] To put the matter a different way, probable cause is needed when a police officer

1. requests an arrest warrant,
2. requests a search warrant,
3. performs a search within a warrant exception, or
4. makes an arrest without an arrest warrant.

So, based on "the totality of the circumstances," the police officer has to explain the elements that give rise to probable cause.

As discussed in chapter two, the test to determine probable cause is, based on the "totality of the circumstances," would the reasonably objective police officer have a strong belief that a crime was committed and that the person to be arrested committed the offense? (This is the test for probable cause to arrest.) For a search, the test is, based on "the totality of the circumstances," would the reasonably objective police officer have a strong belief that specific items will be found in the place to be searched?[59]

At least one court has defined probable cause to mean "a fair probability that contraband or evidence of a crime will be found."[60]

Examples of Probable Cause to Arrest

1. The police officer witnesses a crime.
2. The subject has a warrant.
3. The subject admits to committing a crime.
4. There is a credible victim with corroborating evidence.[61]
5. An illegal weapon is found during a frisk.[62]
6. Narcotics are found during a frisk (plain feel doctrine).[63]
7. The subject was driving without a valid driver's license.[64]

---

[58] *Illinois v. Gates,* 462 U.S. 213 (1983).

[59] *Id.*; *Ornelas,* 517U.S. 690 (Combining these two cases produces the test for a search warrant.).

[60] *United States v. Sokolow,* 490 U.S. 1, 7 (1989) (The Supreme Court is quoting *Illinois,* 462 U.S. 213.).

[61] Corroborating evidence can be witnesses, physical evidence, or observations made by the police officer.

[62] Without valid consent to the frisk, justification (reasonable articulable suspicion) is required for the seizure.

[63] There is a plain feel law that will be discussed later.

Again, probable cause is the amount of evidence that is required by the Fourth Amendment for (1) an arrest warrant, (2) an arrest, (3) a search warrant, or (4) a search without a warrant (when there is a warrant exception).

Probable Cause for a Search

There is probable cause for a search warrant when, based on "the totality of the circumstances," there is a fair probability that contraband or evidence will be found in the location to be searched.[65] (The contraband or evidence of criminal activity has to be described with particularity; the search warrant is not a fishing expedition for evidence of wrong doing.)[66]

So, the police officer has to show that there is a fair probability, based on "the totality of the circumstances," that a specific item will be found in a specific location. To accomplish this, the officer simply explains all the information that is available. Notice how probable cause is explained—articulated—in the following Supreme Court cases.[67]

Carroll v. United States

Even though this case was decided in 1925, it is still good law regarding automobile searches. This incident occurred during the prohibition era. (There was a time when liquor was illegal—the Eighteenth Amendment.) Because liquor was illegal, there was a market for the illegal sale of alcohol. Additionally, police officers and federal agents were on the "lookout" for the manufacture and sale of liquor.

---

[64] In this example, justification for the stop is required. For example, the driver committed a traffic infraction and was pulled over therefor. And the investigation revealed that the driver did not have a valid driver's license. (The driver did not have a valid driver's license.)

[65] *Illinois,* 462 U.S. at 238 (Probable cause is based on "the totality of the circumstances.") See *Brinegar,* 338 U.S. at 175 ("[F]actual and practical considerations of everyday life" can be used to establish probable cause.).

[66] U.S. Const. amend. IV.

[67] *Carroll v. United States,* 267 U.S. 132 (1925); *Brinegar,* 338 U.S. 160.

So, federal officers stopped the car in which Carroll was riding in. Because the officers had previously seen the car in an area known for transporting illegal liquor, suspected that Carroll was involved in the illegal liquor market, and Carroll had offered to sell illegal liquor to undercover federal agents—the said liquor was not delivered, the officers detained the car in which Carroll was in. Thereafter, the agents proceeded to search the car; they tore the rear seat and found illegal liquor under it. Consequently, Carroll was arrested.

The case reached the Supreme Court of the United States (this is the highest court in the land—it is the ultimate authority). The Supreme Court had to decide whether the officers acted unlawfully in searching the car because they did not have a warrant. So, the question before the court was whether officers needed a warrant to search a car that was seized on the roadway. The court concluded that the officers had probable cause to search:

(1) the car was observed in an area known for trafficking of illegal liquor,
(2) Carroll was suspected being involved in the illegal liquor trade (had a neighborhood reputation as a bootlegger), and
(3) Carroll had offered to sell illegal liquor to undercover federal agents.

The arrestee argued that the arrest was illegal because it was the product of an illegal search.

Moreover, the court stated that there was a necessary distinction between an automobile and a private dwelling (a car is different from a house). With this in mind, the court said that because a car is movable and the evidence might escape the officers if the car is driven away, officers can search a car that is seized on the roadway, provided that the officers have probable cause for the search.

In summary, this case is important because it allows police officers to search, without a warrant, a car that is seized on the roadway. But the officers do need probable cause to perform the search. In other words, this case gives police officers more authority to perform their duties because they no longer need a search warrant for a car that is seized on the street. Again, it is important to repeat that officers still need probable cause to execute the search.

Brinegar v. U.S. 1949

An investigator for the Alcohol Tax Unit and a special investigator

(1) observed Brinegar driving towards an area that was known for illegal alcohol smuggling.
(2) Brinegar's car appeared to be weighed down, carrying a heavy load.
(3) Malsed, the investigator, recognized Brinegar because he had arrested him earlier for transporting alcohol across state lines.
(4) Additionally, Malsed had information, through hearsay, that Brinegar was involved in alcohol hauling.[68]
(5) Moreover, Malsed testified that he had observed Brinegar load alcohol on a different vehicle, on an earlier day.

Consequently, Malsed gave chase.

Initially, Brinegar sped off and attempted to elude the officers. Malsed overtook Brinegar and cut him off. Brinegar was forced to stop. Thereafter, Malsed asked Brinegar if he was transporting alcohol. And Brinegar admitted that he was transporting alcohol. A search of the car ensued; and alcohol was found. Brinegar was arrested for illegally transporting alcohol.

Eventually, the case reached the Supreme Court of The United States. The question before the court was whether the officers had probable cause to search the car based on the aforementioned five factors. (At that time the investigatory detention did not exist. So, officers needed probable cause—a higher standard than reasonable suspicion—to pull the car over.)[69] The court stated that the officers had probable cause to stop the car regardless of whether or not Brinegar had admitted to the transportation of alcohol.

This case makes it clear that hearsay evidence can be used for the purpose of probable cause. Additionally, the court stated that an arrest history has probative value and can be used, along with other factors, to establish probable cause. Moreover, the court explained that probable cause was less than what is required to obtain a conviction and more than a mere suspicion.

---

[68] *Brinegar,* 361 U.S. at 173-74 (The Supreme Court stated that hearsay evidence can be used as a factor to establish probable cause. The Supreme Court explained that the rules, for establishing probable cause, are different from the rules for proving guilt "beyond a reasonable doubt.).

[69] *Terry,* 392 U.S. 1 (1968) (Before *Terry*, the investigatory stop did not exist. A seizure required probable cause.).

And, as seen in the two previous cases, that is how probable cause is proven. The officer explains as much information as he or she has available. Also, as mentioned before, probable cause is based on normal everyday observations; probable cause is not a complicated legal analysis. To further explain how non-technical probable cause is, here is another example.

State v. Fisher (2007)

A detective suspected that methamphetamine was being manufactured at a certain location. Consequently, the detective obtained a search warrant. The Supreme Court of Kansas said that there was enough information for a valid search warrant. The detective explained a few factors in the request for a search warrant.

1. A citizen complained that, when trash was burned, there was a peculiar smell.

2. The detective observed Heet bottles on the premises (in the curtilage). According to the detective, this chemical is used in the manufacture of methamphetamine.

3. The officer smelled a strong odor of ether (an odor that is present during the manufacture of methamphetamine) coming from the building.

4. And the detective explained that there was a heavy amount of traffic to and from the location.

Based on the above factors, the court stated that there was probable cause for a search warrant.[70]

So, as evident in the previous three cases, probable cause is proven by explaining facts; and the more factors that are articulated, the more likely that probable cause exists. (As the number of factors goes up, the chances increase that a judge will approve a search warrant.)

---

[70] *State v. Fisher,* 283 Kan. 272 (2007) (There was an additional factor (a garbage bag with incriminating evidence) that the court said was inadmissible because it was obtained through an invalid search of the curtilage. But the court said that the remaining four factors (discussed above) are enough for probable cause.)

Circumstances When an Arrest without a Warrant is Authorized

A police officer is authorized to make an arrest without a warrant when the police officer has probable cause (some states refer to probable cause as reasonable grounds) to believe that the person to be arrested is committing or has committed a crime. Also, a police officer may make a warrantless arrest when there is probable cause to believe that the person to be arrested is wanted on a warrant. Some states have clarified these circumstances into statutes; for example, Illinois enacted 725 ILCS 5/107-2.

> Sec. 107-2. *Arrest by Peace Officer.*
> (1) A peace officer may arrest a person when:
>
> (a) He has a warrant commanding that such person be arrested; or
> (b) He has reasonable grounds to believe that a warrant for the person's arrest has been issued in this State or in another jurisdiction; or
> (c) He has reasonable grounds to believe that the person is committing or has committed an offense.
>
> (2) Whenever a peace officer arrests a person, the officer shall question the arrestee as to whether he or she has any children under the age of 18 living with him or her who may be neglected as a result of the arrest or otherwise. The peace officer shall assist the arrestee in the placement of the children with a relative or other responsible person designated by the arrestee. If the peace officer has reasonable cause to believe that a child may be a neglected child as defined in the Abused and Neglected Child Reporting Act, he shall report it immediately to the Department of Children and Family Services as provided in that Act.
>
> (3) A peace officer who executes a warrant of arrest in good faith beyond the geographical limitation of the warrant shall not be liable for false arrest.[71]

The statute refers to probable cause as reasonable grounds; the term "reasonable grounds" does not have the same meaning as reasonable suspicion. (reasonable suspicion is not enough evidence for an arrest.)

---

[71] See 725 ILCS 5/107-2 (source: P.A. 86-298; 97 -97—333, & 555).

Diagram 4.1

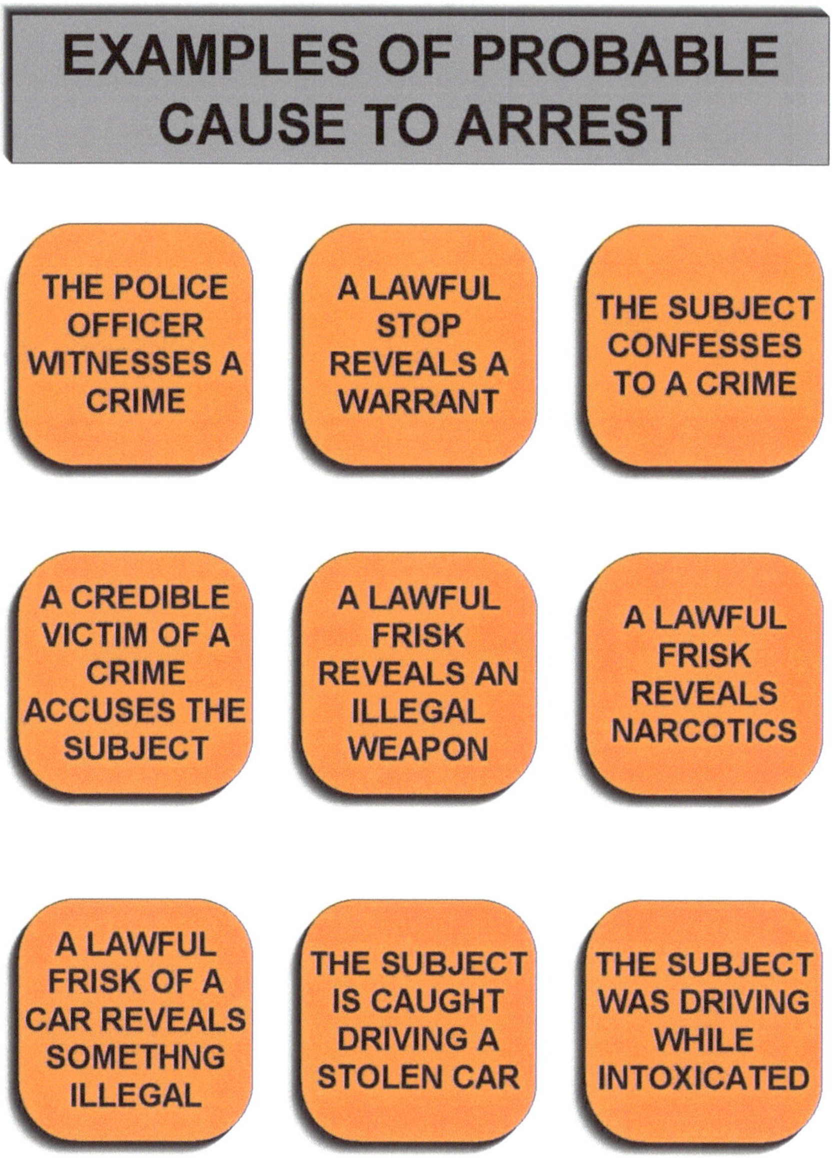
EXAMPLES OF PROBABLE CAUSE TO ARREST
THE POLICE OFFICER WITNESSES A CRIME
A LAWFUL STOP REVEALS A WARRANT
THE SUBJECT CONFESSES TO A CRIME
A CREDIBLE VICTIM OF A CRIME ACCUSES THE SUBJECT
A LAWFUL FRISK REVEALS AN ILLEGAL WEAPON
A LAWFUL FRISK REVEALS NARCOTICS
A LAWFUL FRISK OF A CAR REVEALS SOMETHNG ILLEGAL
THE SUBJECT IS CAUGHT DRIVING A STOLEN CAR
THE SUBJECT WAS DRIVING WHILE INTOXICATED

Review

<u>Objectives</u>:

1. Define search warrant.

- A search warrant is a judge approved order that authorizes the search of a location for specific items. As required by the Fourth Amendment, probable cause is needed for a search warrant. Probable cause is established by "the totality of the circumstances."[72] **According to 725 ILCS 5/108-7, a search warrant is a court issued order:**

  - **[t]he warrant shall command the person directed to execute the same to search the place or person particularly described in the warrant and to seize the instruments, articles or things particularly described in the warrant.**[73]

[72] *Illinois,* 462 U.S. 213.

[73] See 725 ILCS 5/108-7 (citing Laws 1968, p. 2836). The boldface was added by the author. This is the definition of a search warrant in Illinois. The definitions in other states might vary. But the overall idea is the same; a search warrant is an order from a judge that authorizes the search of a location for specific items.

2. Define contraband.

➢ Contraband is an item that is illegal to possess. For example, a person carrying an illegal firearm (e.g. unregistered). The Supreme Court said that carrying contraband is illegal.[74] Sometimes an item is contraband because the citizen has not met certain criteria. To elaborate, carrying a firearm might be legal in a certain city; but carrying an unregistered pistol might be illegal in that same city. (So, the carrying of the unregistered gun amounts to possessing contraband.) To repeat, contraband is something that is illegal to possess. Many items are contraband; here are a few examples:

- illegal drugs (for example, marijuana, cocaine, methamphetamine),
- illegal weapons (for example, assault weapons, sawed-off shotguns),
- child pornography,
- counterfeit money, and
- obscene material for public distribution. (The Supreme Court has not defined what obscene material is; Justice Stewart stated that "I know it when I see it.")[75]

---

[74] *Illinois v. Caballes,* 543 U.S. 405, 408 (2005) (The Supreme Court said "We have held that any interest in possessing contraband cannot be deemed 'legitimate....'").
[75] *Jacobellis v. Ohio,* 378 U.S. 184 (1964).

3. Identify elements giving rise to probable cause.

➢ According to the Fourth Amendment to the United States, "no warrants shall issue but upon probable cause."[76] Probable cause is the standard of proof that is required by the Fourth Amendment for a warrant or an arrest.[77] This means that the police officer has to explain evidence that amounts to probable cause. Additionally, the police officer is allowed to use "the totality of the circumstances" to prove probable cause.[78] These are examples of the factors (sometimes referred to as elements) that a police officer is allowed to use for establishing probable cause:

- personal observation,
- person's behavior (e.g. nervousness, contradicting statements, and evasiveness—flight), and
- location (e.g. heavy narcotics area, area known for robberies, and an area where people get shot).

4. Recognize circumstances when an arrest without a warrant is authorized.

➢ A police officer is authorized to make an arrest without a warrant when the police officer has probable cause (some states refer to probable cause as reasonable grounds) to believe that the person to be arrested is committing or has committed a crime. Also, a police officer may make a warrantless arrest when there is probable cause to believe that the person to be arrested is wanted on a warrant. (Some states have clarified these circumstances into statutes; for example, Illinois enacted 725 ILCS 5/107-2.)

---

[76] U.S. Const. amend. IV.

[77] *Id.*

[78] *Illinois,* 462 U.S. 213.

Conclusion

Under the "totality of the circumstances" approach, a police officer is allowed to use a wide variety of information to establish probable cause for an arrest or a search. The officer is allowed to use the person's arrest record, hearsay information, personal experience, special training, and location. (On a related topic, these factors (also called elements) can be used to establish reasonable suspicion for a seizure or a frisk.) The following chapters contain more explanations and examples of these topics.

Review Questions

1. Define search warrant. ________________________________

____

____

2. What is the standard of proof that is needed for a search warrant?

____

____

3. Give examples of factors (also called elements) that a police officer can use to establish probable cause. __________________

____

____

4. Define contraband. ____________________________________

____

____

5. Give examples of contraband. ____________________________

____

____

6. Explain what probable cause means. ________________________

____

____

7. When is an arrest without a warrant authorized? ______________

____

____

____

Notes

Date:

Notes

Date:

Notes

Date:

Notes

Date:

Chapter 5

Probable Cause, Arrest Warrants, and Arrests

Objectives:

The student will be able to

1. identify the proper procedures for taking into custody persons detained by a citizen,
2. identify the procedures for obtaining an arrest warrant,
3. identify the requisites of an arrest warrant,
4. identify the procedures for executing an arrest warrant,
5. identify the legal procedures to follow upon arrest of suspect, and
6. recognize the circumstances where a peace officer may release an arrested person.

Arrests

One of the duties of a police officer is to arrest people. Against that background, a police officer will arrest people for crimes that the police officer witnesses. Sometimes the police officer will arrest a person due to an outstanding arrest warrant. Other times, a police officer will arrest a person based on credible information from a victim of a crime.

Proper Procedure for Taking Into custody Persons Detained by a Citizen

If a citizen detains a person until the police arrive, then it is still the responsibility of the police officers to determine if there is probable cause to arrest for a criminal act. If the police officer determines that there is probable cause to arrest, then the police officer arrests the person. Additionally, if the person who was holding the law breaker witnessed the crime, then the police officer should document the identity of the witness. (Courts assume that, absent any indication of lying, that citizens who volunteer information to the police are being truthful;[79] but corroborating the citizen's statements will increase the amount of probable cause.)

Procedures for Obtaining an Arrest Warrant

The requirements for getting an arrest warrant vary from state to state. And the requirements are spelled out in the state's law (in a statute). Also, some police departments require the approval of a state's attorney before the complaint—also called an affidavit—is presented to a judge. But in all cases, it is a judge who issues an arrest warrant. The judge looks at the available evidence (including examining available witnesses) and determines whether or not there is probable cause to issue an arrest warrant. As mentioned before, the procedures for obtaining an arrest warrant vary from state to state. In Illinois, for example, according to 725 ILCS 5/107-9, a written complaint with specific information is required.

> (1) When a complaint is presented to a court charging that an offense has been committed it shall examine upon oath or affirmation the complainant or any witnesses.
>
> (b) The complaint shall be in writing and shall:
>
> (1) State the name of the accused if known, and if not known the accused may be designated by any name or description by which he can be identified with reasonable certainty;
>
> (2) State the offense with which the accused is charged;
>
> (3) State the time and place of the offense as definitely as can be done by the complainant; and
>
> (4) Be subscribed and sworn to by the complainant.[80]

These are the minimum legal requirements in Illinois.

---

[79] *United States v. Scalia,* 993 F.2d 984 (1st Cir. 1993).

[80] See 725 ILCS 5/107-9 (citing P.A. 86-298; 87-523).

Requisites of an Arrest Warrant

An arrest warrant is an order from a judge that orders the arrest of a person. (The requisites of an arrest warrant—which are determined by state law—will vary from state to state.) In Illinois, for example, state law gives the requirements of an arrest warrant.

(1) Be in writing;

(2) Specify the name, sex and birth date of the person to be arrested or if his name, sex or birth date is unknown, shall designate such person by any name or description by which he can be identified with reasonable certainty;

(3) Set forth the nature of the offense;

(4) State the date when issued and the municipality or county where issued;

(5) Be signed by the judge of the court with the title of his office;

(6) Command that the person against whom the complaint was made be arrested and brought before the court issuing the warrant or if he is absent or unable to act before the nearest or most accessible court in the same county;

(7) Specify the amount of bail; and

(8) Specify any geographical limitation placed on the execution of the warrant, but such limitation shall not be expressed in mileage.

(e) The warrant shall be directed to all peace officers in the State. It shall be executed by the peace officer, or by a private person specially named therein, at any location within the geographic limitation for execution placed on the warrant. If no geographic limitation is placed on the warrant, then it may be executed anywhere in the state.[81]

Procedures for Executing an Arrest Warrant

The procedures for executing an arrest warrant are controlled by state law and Supreme Court cases. For example, in Illinois, the warrant is "directed to all peace officers,"[82] a private person may be commanded to make the arrest, the warrant may list the geographical boundaries, and if no boundaries are specified, then the warrant is valid anywhere in the state of Illinois.[83]

Additionally, related to executing an arrest warrant, an arrest warrant may be executed on the public way. The Supreme Court has addressed the issues about executing arrest warrants in different locations.

1. An arrest warrant may be executed on the public way.[84]
2. A search warrant is not required when an arrest warrant is executed in the arrestee's home.[85]
3. **Absent exigent circumstances, a search warrant is required (for a non-consensual search) to arrest the person named in the warrant inside a third party's residence.[86]**

So, to be clear, even though there is an arrest warrant on a person, a search warrant might be needed if the person is inside a third party's home.

Legal Procedures to Follow Upon Arrest of a Suspect

As long as the arrestee is not being questioned about a crime, the *Miranda* warnings are not required. But if the arrestee is questioned about a crime, then the

---

[81] See 725 ILCS 5/107-9 (quoting P.A. 86-298; 87-523).
[82] See 725 ILCS 5/107-9 (e) (quoting P.A. 86-298; 87-523).
[83] *Id.*
[84] *Unites States v. Watson,* 423 U.S. 411, (414-417) (Police officers are allowed to make arrests on the public way—based on probable cause—without approval from a court; an arrest warrant is probable cause to arrest.).
[85] *Payton v. New York,* 445 U.S. 573,603 (1980) (The Supreme Court held that "an arrest warrant founded on probable cause implicitly carries with it the limited authority to enter a dwelling in which the suspect lives when there is reason to believe the suspect is within.").
[86] *Steagald v. United States,* 451 U.S. 204, 216 (1981) (Absent consent and without exigent circumstances, a search warrant is required to execute a warrant inside a third party's residence.).

Miranda warnings must be given.[87] Additionally, the arrestee is entitled to other due process rights—guaranteed by the constitution; these rights are sometimes spelled out in a state statute. For example, in Illinois, according to 725 ILCS 5/109-1, the statute says that an arrestee shall be allowed to see a judge without unnecessary delay.

> A person arrested with or without a warrant shall be taken without unnecessary delay before the nearest and most accessible judge in that county, except when such county is a participant in a regional jail authority, in which event such person may be taken to the nearest and most accessible judge, irrespective of the county where such judge presides, and a charge shall be filed. Whenever a person arrested either with or without a warrant is required to be taken before a judge, a charge may be filed against such person by way of a two-way closed circuit television system, except that a hearing to deny bail to the defendant may not be conducted by way of closed circuit television.[88]

So, in Illinois, according to the above statute, after an arrest is made, an arrestee is entitled to

1. see a judge, without unnecessary delay, in the county of arrest,
2. if it is an out of county warrant, then the arrestee is entitled to see a judge in the county of arrest,
3. having charges filed, and
4. the protections of the rights that are guaranteed by statute.

So, charges have to be filed without undue delay. And the arrestee is entitled to see a judge without undue delay.

---

[87] *Miranda v. Arizona,* 384 U.S. 436, 469 (1966) (The Supreme Court stated that custodial interrogation requires the warnings that are now called the *Miranda* warnings.).
[88] See 725 ILCS 5/109-1 (a) (quoting P.A. 90-14, eff. 1-1-98).

Circumstances when a Peace Officer May Release an Arrested Person

Sometimes a peace officer will make an arrest only to realize that there is no probable cause to charge the arrestee. In other words, the officer realizes that there are no grounds for a criminal complaint against the arrestee and the arrest was made without a warrant. For example, according to 725 ILCS 5/107-6, in Illinois, this authority is spelled out in a statute.

> A peace officer who arrests a person without a warrant is authorized to release the person without requiring him to appear before a court when the officer is satisfied that there are no grounds for criminal complaint against the person arrested.[89]

Even though the person was released without charging, the person was still, under the Fourth Amendment, subject to the full-blown custodial arrest. For this reason, some police departments require the police officer to complete the arrest (paperwork, photos, fingerprints and so on) and release without charging.

Review

Objectives:

1. Identify the proper procedures for taking into custody persons detained by a citizen.

- If a citizen detains a person until the police arrive, then it is still the responsibility of the police officers to determine if there is probable cause to arrest for a criminal act. If the police officer determines that there is probable cause to arrest, then the police officer arrests the person. Additionally, if the person who was holding the law breaker witnessed the crime, then the police officer should document the identity of the witness.

[89] See 725 ILCS 5/107-6 (quoting Laws 1963, p. 2836).

2. Identify the procedures for obtaining an arrest warrant.

- It is a judge who issues an arrest warrant. The judge looks at the available evidence (including examining available witnesses) and determines whether or not there is probable cause to issue an arrest warrant. As mentioned before, the procedures for obtaining an arrest warrant vary from state to state. In Illinois, for example, according to 725 ILCS 5/107-9, a written complaint with specific information is required.

> (a) When a complaint is presented to a court charging that an offense has been committed it shall examine upon oath or affirmation the complainant or any witnesses.
>
> (b) The complaint shall be in writing and shall:
>
> (1) State the name of the accused if known, and if not known the accused may be designated by any name or description by which he can be identified with reasonable certainty;
>
> (2) State the offense with which the accused is charged;
>
> (3) State the time and place of the offense as definitely as can be done by the complainant; and
>
> (4) Be subscribed and sworn to by the complainant.[90]

[90] See 725 ILCS 5/107-9 (citing P.A. 86-298; 87-523).

3. Identify the requisites of an arrest warrant.

- An arrest warrant is an order from a judge that commands the arrest of a person. (The requisites of an arrest warrant—which are determined by state law—will vary from state to state.) In Illinois, for example, state law gives the requirements of an arrest warrant.

  (1) Be in writing;

  (2) Specify the name, sex and birth date of the person to be arrested or if his name, sex or birth date is unknown, shall designate such person by any name or description by which he can be identified with reasonable certainty;

  (3) Set forth the nature of the offense;

  (4) State the date when issued and the municipality;

  (5) Be signed by the judge of the court with the title of his office;

  (6) Command that the person against whom the complaint was made be arrested and brought before the court issuing the warrant or if he is absent or unable to act before the nearest or most accessible court in the same county;

  (e) The warrant shall be directed to all peace officers in the State. It shall be executed by the peace officer, or by a private person specially named therein, at any location within the geographic limitation for execution placed on the warrant. If no geographic limitation is placed on the warrant, then it may be executed anywhere in the state.[91]

[91] See 725 ILCS 5/107-9 (quoting P.A. 86-298; 87-523).

4. Identify the procedures for executing an arrest warrant.

➢ The procedures for executing an arrest warrant are controlled by state law and Supreme Court cases. For example, in Illinois, the warrant is "directed to all peace officers,"[92] a private person may be commanded to make the arrest, the warrant may list the geographical boundaries, and if no boundaries are specified, then the warrant is valid anywhere in the state of Illinois.[93]

- An arrest warrant may be executed on the public way.[94]
- A search warrant is not required when an arrest warrant is executed in the arrestee's home.[95]
- **Absent exigent circumstances, a search warrant is required (for a non-consensual search) to arrest the person named in the warrant inside a third party's residence.**[96]

5. Identify the legal procedures to follow upon arrest of suspect.

➢ An arrestee is entitled to due process rights, these rights are sometimes spelled out in the state's statute, for example, in Illinois, an arrestee is entitled to

5. see a judge, without unnecessary delay, in the county of arrest,
6. if it is an out of county warrant, then the arrestee is entitled to see a judge in the county of arrest,
7. having charges filed, and
8. the protections of the rights that are guaranteed by statute.

---

[92] See 725 ILCS 5/107-9 (e) (quoting P.A. 86-298; 87-523).
[93] *Id.*
[94] *Unites States v. Watson,* 423 U.S. 411, (414-417) (Police officers are allowed to make arrests on the public way—based on probable cause—without approval from a court; an arrest warrant is probable cause to arrest.).
[95] *Payton v. New York,* 445 U.S. 573,603 (1980) (The Supreme Court held that "an arrest warrant founded on probable cause implicitly carries with it the limited authority to enter a dwelling in which the suspect lives when there is reason to believe the suspect is within.").
[96] *Steagald v. United States,* 451 U.S. 204, 216 (1981) (Absent consent and without exigent circumstances, a search warrant is required to execute a warrant inside a third party's residence.).

Therefore, charges must be filed without undue delay. In addition, the arrestee is entitled to see a judge without undue delay.[97]

5. Recognize the circumstances where a peace officer may release an arrested person.

- Sometimes a peace officer will make an arrest only to realize that there is no probable cause to charge the arrestee. In other words, the officer realizes that there are no grounds for a criminal complaint against the arrestee and the arrest was made without a warrant. For example, according to 725 ILCS 5/107-6, in Illinois, this authority is spelled out in a statute.

    - A peace officer who arrests a person without a warrant is authorized to release the person without requiring him to appear before a court when the officer is satisfied that there are no grounds for criminal complaint against the person arrested.[98]

Conclusion

A police officer has to be aware of where an arrest warrant may be executed. Additionally, a police officer has to have an understanding of probable cause. As discussed before, probable cause is not a complicated concept, but it is a very important part of law enforcement. (For a review of probable cause, read the cases in Chapter Four: *Carroll v. United States*, *Brinegar v. United States*, and *State v. Fisher*.) Also, similar to and related to probable cause, reasonable suspicion is a crucial concept that should be mastered by police officers. In Chapter Six, reasonable suspicion and probable cause are discussed in further detail; more examples, explanations, discussions, and cases follow.

[97] See 725 ILCS 5/109-1 (a) (quoting P.A. 90-14, eff. 1-1-98).
[98] See 725 ILCS 5/107-6 (quoting Laws 1963, p. 2836).

Review Questions

1. What must a police officer do when taking a person detained by a citizen into custody? ____
____
____
____

2. Identify the procedures for obtaining an arrest warrant.
____
____
____
____

3. Identify the requisites of an arrest warrant. ____________________
____
____
____
____

4. Identify the procedures for executing an arrest warrant. _________
____
____
____
____

5. May an officer execute an arrest warrant on the public way? _____
____

Review Questions

6. Identify the legal procedures to follow upon the arrest of a person.

____

____

____

____

7. When may a peace officer release an arrested person? __________

____

____

____

8. Does a police officer need a search warrant to execute an arrest warrant inside the home of the person who is named in the arrest warrant? Can you name a case to support your position? ________

____

____

____

9. Does a police officer, absent exigent circumstances, need a search warrant to execute an arrest warrant in the home of a third party? Can you name a case that supports your answer? ______________

____

____

10. May an officer release a person arrested on a valid warrant? _____

Notes

Date:

Notes

Date:

Notes

Date:

Notes

Date:

Notes

Date:

Notes

Date:

Chapter 6

Seizures, Frisks, Plain Feel, and Search Warrants

Objectives:

The student will be able to

1. recognize when a stop is authorized,
2. recognize when a frisk is authorized,
3. understand the "Plain Feel" law, and
4. recognize when a search warrant is required.

The seizure—a stop—and the frisk, a limited search for weapons, were discussed earlier. The practical aspect of how to explain (or justify) the stop and frisk will be covered in this chapter. Additionally, the "Plain Feel" law, which is related to the frisk, will be covered. Furthermore, circumstances when a search warrant is required will be discussed.

The Stop (The *Terry* Stop)

The stop is also known as the *Terry* stop.[99] A stop is a seizure and the subject is not free to leave. This type of police/citizen encounter requires reasonable articulable suspicion that criminal activity is afoot.[100] Put another way, the police officer has to explain why the stop was made. Also, during the stop, if the police officer has reasonable articulable suspicion that the subject is "presently armed and dangerous," then the police officer may legally perform a frisk—a limited search for weapons.[101]

---

[99] *Terry v. Ohio,* 392 U.S. 1 (1969) (This case created the investigatory detention—the stop—for police officers; prior to this case, without probable cause, a police officer could not legally seize a person.) *Brinegar,* 338 U.S. at 178-179 (In 1948, the concurring judge, Justice Burton, argued that police officers should be allowed to conduct investigatory stops; it took nineteen years for the investigatory stop to materialize.).

[100] *Terry,* 392 U.S. at 29-30 (The Supreme Court stated that, because the officer had reasonable articulable suspicion that a robbery was about to be committed, both the seizure and the frisk were reasonable and legal.).

[101] *Id.*

Diagram 6.1[102]

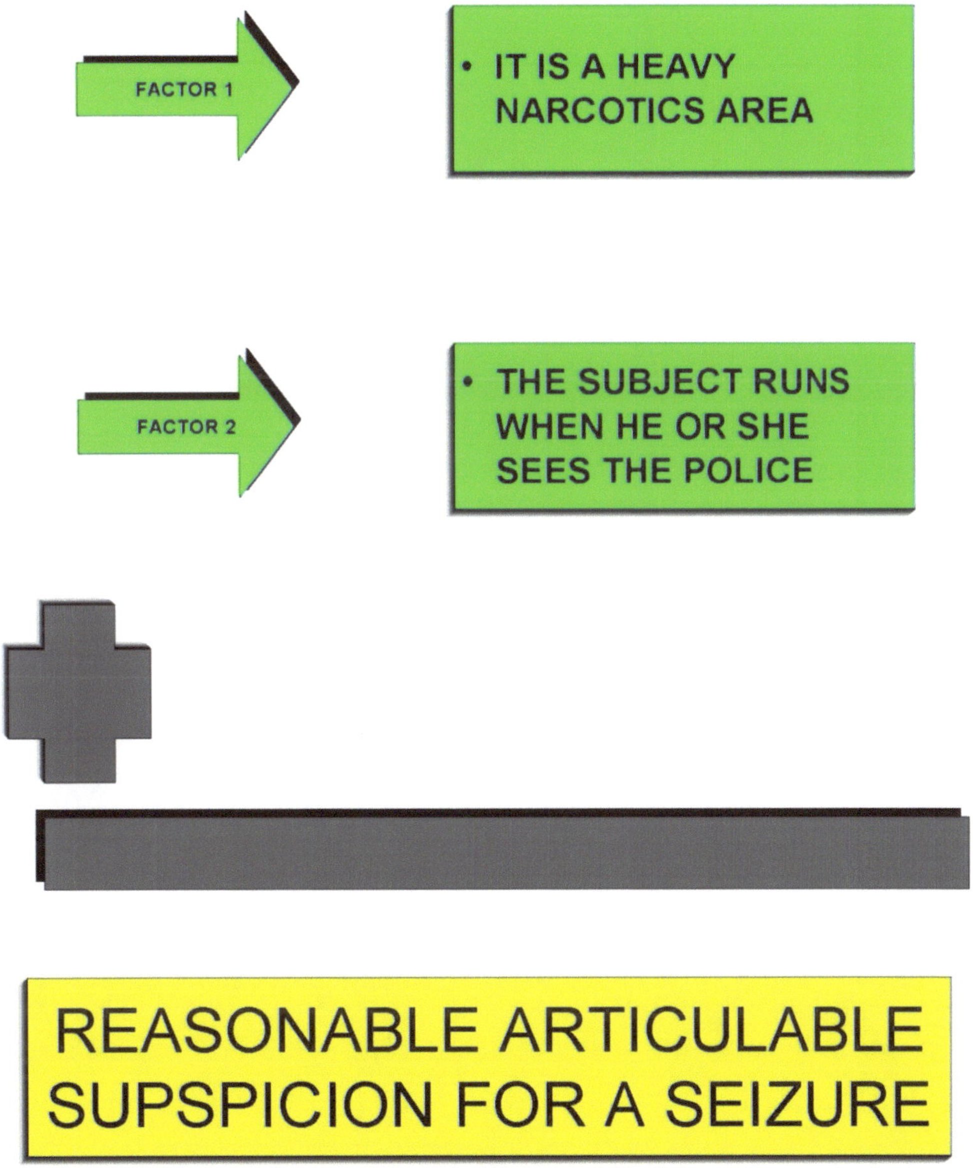

[102] See *Illinois v. Wardlow,* 528 U.S. 119 (2000) (The Supreme Court ruled that these two factors are enough for a seizure.).

Brown v. Texas (1979)[103]

While patrolling in a heavy narcotics area, at about noon, two police officers observed two men meet in an alley. Thereafter, the officers detained one of the men, Brown; the officers frisked Brown for weapons and asked him to identify himself. Brown refused to identify himself. Thereafter, the officers arrested Brown for refusing to identify himself.

A Texan statute made it a crime for a person who had been lawfully stopped to refuse to identify himself or herself. The officers testified that they detained Brown because the situation, in the alley—two men meeting, looked suspicious. The officers, however, did not state what criminal activity they suspected Brown of being engaged in. Brown contested that the officers had no right to stop him. The case eventually reached the Supreme Court of the United States ("the Supreme Court").

The question before the Supreme Court was whether the officers had reasonable articulable suspicion to stop and detain Brown. This question involves the Fourth Amendment. The Fourth Amendment requires that seizures be reasonable.[104] In other words, was the seizure reasonable?

Officer Venegas (one of the arresting officers) testified at the trial that the situation looked suspicious. Officer Venegas, however, did not point to any facts to support the assertion that the situation looked suspicious.[105] Consequently, the Supreme Court ruled that the seizure was unlawful.

In conclusion, the lesson from this case is that the police officer has to give the facts that make the situation suspicious. Therefore, the officer has to explain why he or she performed (1) the stop and (2) the frisk. It is not enough for the officer to merely say that the situation looked suspicious.[106]

---

[103] *Id.*

[104] *United States v. Brignoni-Ponce,* 422 U.S. 873, 878 (1975) (The Supreme Court Stated that a stop has to be reasonable; in other words, the police officer has to say why the situation looked suspicious.).

[105] *Brown,* 443 U.S. at 52.

[106] *Brown v. Texas,* 443 U.S. 47, 50 (1979) (The Supreme Court ruled that a stop that is not supported by objective facts of criminal activity violates the Fourth Amendment; in this case the officer testified that the situation looked suspicious, at 52; but the officer did not supply any factors to support the suspiciousness of the event.).

Diagram 6.2

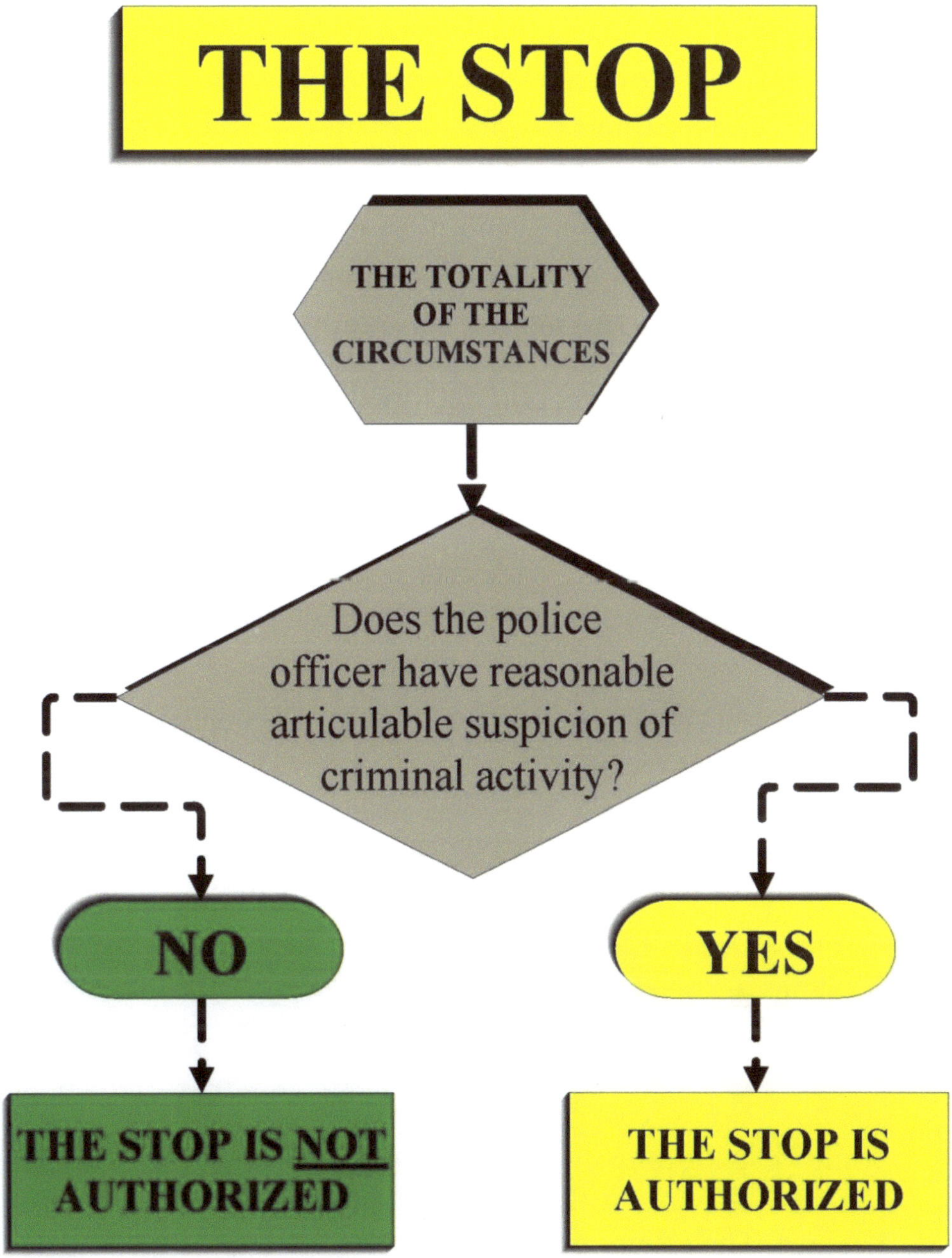
THE STOP
THE TOTALITY OF THE CIRCUMSTANCES
Does the police officer have reasonable articulable suspicion of criminal activity?
NO
YES
THE STOP IS NOT AUTHORIZED
THE STOP IS AUTHORIZED

In addition to the Supreme Court cases that explain when a stop is authorized, some states have made the authority of police officers to perform stops state law. For example, Illinois enacted statute 725 ILCS 5/107-14.

> Temporary questioning without arrest. **A peace officer, after having identified himself as a peace officer, may stop any person in a public place for a reasonable period of time when the officer reasonably infers from the circumstances that the person is committing, is about to commit or has committed an offense as defined in Section 102-15 of this Code, and may demand the name and address of the person and an explanation of his actions. Such detention and temporary questioning will be conducted in the vicinity of where the person was stopped.**[107]

Again, the officer has to point to specific factors that support why the situation was suspicious.

> Example 6.1: Because the officer was (1) patrolling in a high robbery area, (2) observed the subject standing on the sidewalk and looking into a store, (3) businesses were about to close, (4) and the subject remained in the same spot for 15 minutes—it was not a bus stop, the officer performed a stop on the subject to investigate whether or not a robbery was in motion.[108]

In the above example, the officer gave four factors (or four reasons) to support the investigatory stop. These four factors explain why the situation looked suspicious. In other words, these four factors explain why the officer reasonably inferred that the subject was about to commit a crime. Notice how this is different from merely stating that the situation looked suspicious.

> Example 6.2: The officer performed a stop on the subject because, while (1) patrolling in a heavy narcotics neighborhood, the subject, who was standing still, (2) took flight upon the officer's presence in the area. The officer wanted to make sure that the subject was not involved in criminal activity.[109]

---

[107] See 725 ILCS 5/107-14 (quoting Laws 1968, p. 218) (The boldface was added by the author.).

[108] See *Terry,* 392 U.S. (The factors in the example are similar to the factors in the case.).

[109] See *Illinois v. Wardlow,* 528 U.S. 119 (2000) (The Supreme Court stated that a person running upon the presence of the police is not enough to perform a stop on the person who ran. But the Supreme Court made it

In the previous example, the officer gave two factors to justify the stop. And, although running upon the presence of the police is very suspicious, the Supreme Court has said that this one factor alone does not justify a stop; but the two factors that are in example 6.2 are enough for a stop.[110]

> Example 6.3: The officer stopped the subject because, during a face-to-face encounter with a citizen, (1) the citizen told the officer that the subject had a firearm in his waistband and that the subject was looking to rob someone. The officer (2) was patrolling in a high robbery area. The officer stopped the subject to investigate if the subject was planning a robbery.[111]

In the above example, the police officer gave two factors for the stop. Notice how this is different from merely saying that the situation looked suspicious. In all three examples (6.1, 6.2, and 6.3), the officer could reasonably infer that a crime was about to be committed, was being committed, or had just being committed. To explain the matter another way, the officer had reasonable articulable suspicion—the factors—that criminal activity was afoot.

Additionally, related to factors, the Supreme Court ruled that information from an anonymous caller—without more—is not enough for a stop.[112] But the police officer is still allowed to patrol on the public way; and the officer might observe factors that justify a stop.

> Example 6.4: Dispatch (1) relays information, from an anonymous phone caller, to a police officer that a white male standing on the corner of 6300 S Harlem is carrying a firearm. So, the officer grabs the male and performs a frisk which reveals a firearm.[113]

In the above example, the one factor without any evidence of reliability is not enough for a stop.[114] The one factor, in example 6.4, does not amount to reasonable

---

clear that if the person runs upon the presence of the police and it is in a heavy narcotics neighborhood, then the two factors are enough to perform a stop on the person who ran.).

110 *Id.*

111 See *Adams v. Williams,* 407 U.S. 143, 147 (1990) (The Supreme Court ruled that information obtained from a face-to-face informant can be used as a factor for a stop.).

112 See *Florida v. J.L.,* 529 U.S. 266, 273-274 (2000) (The Supreme Court ruled that information, from an anonymous caller, lacking any information of reliability is not enough for a stop.).

113 *Id.*

114 *Id.*

articulable suspicion for a stop.[115] The cases that follow will give the reader an excellent idea of what constitutes reasonable articulable suspicion for a stop.[116]

United States v. Cortez (1981)[117]

After discovering several sets of footprints, with each set containing a few distinctive patterns in the shape of chevrons, Border Patrol Officers began to suspect that someone was guiding undocumented aliens from Mexico into the United States. Based on the number of shoe prints, the Border Patrol Officers ascertained groups of from 8 to 20 persons had been guided from Mexico into Arizona. The shoe prints led to a highway. Based on the Border Patrol Officers' investigation, the officers reasoned that a truck was picking up the groups of people on the highway.[118]

The truck had to be of a type capable of transporting 8-20 persons, reasoned the officers. Additionally, the officers calculated (based on the amount of time needed to walk the 30 mile journey, the discovery of fresh shoeprints, and the conclusion that the groups travelled on clear nights during or close to weekends) that the vehicle was making the pickups between 2:00 a.m. and 6:00 a.m.

Armed with this information, the officers conducted surveillance with the purpose of investigating vehicles on the road, by the area where the footprints ended, between 2:00 a.m. and 6:00 a.m. that could transport 8-20 people. At 4:30 a.m., the officers spotted a pickup with a camper shell heading west. Subsequently, the officers spotted the same pickup heading east. The officers suspected that the pickup was on its way east because the driver had already lifted the undocumented aliens.

---

[115] There are situations in which an anonymous informant supplies information with enough indicia of reliability to justify a stop.

[116] The Supreme Court has not stated how many factors are required to justify a stop.

[117] *United States v. Cortez,* 449 U.S. 411 (1981) (The Supreme Court ruled that the officers had reasonable suspicion to stop the truck.).

[118] This means that the officers are focused on vehicles that can carry 8-20 people. To elaborate, an economy car that carries at most 4 people is not the subject of the investigation. The officers are not justified in stopping economy cars because there is no connection between the economy car (does not hold 8-20 people) and the human smuggling.

United States v. Cortez

The officers pulled the vehicle over; Hernandez-Loera was riding in the front part of the pickup. Hernandez-Loera was wearing shoes with soles that matched the "chevron" style prints that were found in the desert. The officers, after identifying themselves as police officers, asked Cortez, the driver, if there were any passenger in the back of the truck. Cortez opened the back part of the truck; there were six undocumented people.

Consequently, the officers arrested Hernandez-Loera and Cortez for transporting illegal aliens in violation of 8 U.S.C. §1324(a). The arrestees sought to suppress the evidence; they argued that the officers did not have lawful authority to make the investigative stop. Eventually, the case reached the Supreme Court of the United States ("the Supreme Court").

The question before the Supreme Court was whether the officers had reasonable suspicion to stop the truck. The Supreme Court stated that, in evaluating reasonable suspicion, the totality of the circumstances (the whole picture) must be taken into account. The court also articulated that there must be a suspicion that the person stopped is engaged in criminal activity.[119]

The Supreme Court ruled that the officers had reasonable articulable suspicion to stop the truck.[120] (The officers knew that the area was an illegal aliens smuggling spot; the officers also narrowed down the time-frame for the lifting of the aliens; also, the officers were focused on a specific type of vehicle) In other words, the officers acted lawfully and did not violate the arrestees' Fourth Amendment rights.

In the above case, the officers articulated at least three factors to justify the stop. Additionally, the court said that the stop met the second requirement of the investigatory detention; there must be a connection between the person stopped

---

[119] This is called a second requirement of the stop. The person stopped has to be connected to the suspected criminal activity. (See *Cortez,* 449 U.S. at 418.).

[120] The Supreme Court stated that the stop has to be focused on the person who is suspected of the illegal activity. So, the first part of the test is whether there is reasonable articulable suspicion for the stop. And the second part of the test requires that the person stopped be connected to the suspected activity (see page 418).

and the suspected criminal activity.[121] This means that the officers would not have been justified in stopping every car on the road to investigate human smuggling.

Florida v. J.L.[122]

Acting on an anonymous phone call (about a young black male, wearing a plaid shirt, standing at a specific bus stop, carrying a firearm), police officers detained and patted down J.L.. In addition, the police officers recovered a gun. J.L. fit the description (young black male, wearing a plaid shirt, and standing on a specific bus stop). J.L. requested that the trial court suppress the firearm because it was obtained by an unreasonable seizure and frisk.

The Supreme Court had to decide the question of whether information from an anonymous caller amounts to reasonable suspicion to detain a person and perform a pat down. The court stated that even if the description of the person was accurate, there was not enough information to make the officers suspect that J.L. was involved in criminal activity. Additionally, The Supreme Court reasoned that it was difficult to hold the anonymous caller accountable if the information would have turned out to be false. (In this case, the police officers did not have a recording of the call.) Based on all of this, The Supreme Court ruled that the information from the anonymous caller, without more, was not reasonable articulable suspicion to justify the stop and search.

In summary, based on this case, information, describing a person, from an anonymous caller—without additional facts—is not enough to justify neither a seizure nor a frisk. This means that the police officer has to articulate more than the information gathered from the anonymous caller to justify a seizure and a frisk. For the advanced students, the court mentioned did if the anonymous caller described information beyond the description of the person (for example, the activities of the person) and the officers observed activity that corroborated the information, then the seizure and the frisk might have been justified.[123]

---

[121] *Id.*

[122] *J.L.*, 529 U.S. at 273 (The Supreme Court ruled that anonymous information that lacked indicia of reliability is not enough to justify a stop.).

[123] *Id.* at 273 (This same call might justify a stop at an airport or other high security area.).

Alabama v. White (1990)[124]

Police officers received, through an anonymous phone call, information that White would (1) be leaving an apartment located in the 235 Lynwood Terrace Apartments, (2) would leave at a particular time, (3) would drive a specific vehicle (with a broken taillight), and (4) would go to the Dobey Motel. Additionally, the caller stated that White would be in possession of cocaine. After the call, officers went over to the Lynwood Terrace apartments. Thereafter, the officers noticed a vehicle that matched the description. Additionally, the officers observed White get in the car and drive off. The Officers followed White who was apparently on her way to the Dobey Motel.

Before White reached the Dobey Motel, the officers pulled White over. After White gave the officers consent to search the car, the officers found marijuana inside White's car. White was formally arrested. During a custodial search, the officers found cocaine in White's purse. White was charged with possession of marijuana and possession of cocaine.

At the trial court, White pled guilty, reserving the right to appeal the denial to suppress the evidence. The appeals court reversed White's conviction because, according to the appeals court, the officers did not have reasonable suspicion to seize White. Eventually, the case reached the Supreme Court of the United States.

So, the Supreme Court decided the question of whether the information from the anonymous caller gave the police officers reasonable suspicion to stop White. The Supreme Court, acknowledging that this was a close case, stated that the officers had reasonable suspicion to pull White over because the anonymous caller described White's future behavior:

1. White would be leaving a Lynwood Terrace apartment,
2. White would get into a specific car (with a broken tail lamp),
3. White would be leaving during a stated time-frame, and
4. White would be driving to Dobey's Motel.

[124] *Alabama v. White,* 496 U.S. 325 (1990).

Alabama v. White (1990)

According to the Supreme Court, the aforementioned information contained a sufficient indicia of reliability to amount to reasonable suspicion for an investigatory stop. In other words, the court said that the officers had reasonable suspicion to detain White. In reaching this conclusion, the court applied "The Totality of the Circumstances" test. Additionally, the court said that the quantity and the quality of the information are considered when applying "The Totality of the Circumstances" approach. All of this means that White was legally stopped and the evidence was lawfully obtained.

In summary, in determining whether reasonable suspicion exists, the quality and quantity of the information are considered. Additionally, as the Supreme Court mentioned, observations made by the officers can be used to justify reasonable suspicion. Again, the legal test to apply to anonymous information is "The Totality of the Circumstances" standard. And police officers can add observations to the anonymous information to articulate reasonable suspicion.

The important thing to remember is that the information, from anonymous callers, has to have some indicia of reliability. What is the difference between *J.L.* and *White?* Is the Supreme Court been consistent? Do you agree with the decisions? Keep in mind that stops are not full-blown custodial arrests; they are temporary investigatory detentions. Because stops are brief encounters (seizures) probable cause (the amount of evidence that is needed for a full-blown custodial arrest) is not required. Reasonable articulable suspicion is required.

The Frisk (Pat-Down)

Related to stops, frisks require the same level of proof as stops, reasonable articulable suspicion. This is a separate test. In other words, the police officer has to explain (1) reasonable suspicion that criminal activity is afoot and (2) reasonable suspicion that the subject is presently armed and dangerous. So, just because the stop is justified, it does not necessarily follow that the frisk is justified. The frisk is explained the same way that the stop is explained. The officer lists the factors that justify the frisk. (There are situations in which the same factors that justify the stop justify the frisk.) (See *Terry,* 392 U.S.)

> Example: 6.5: Because the officer was (1) patrolling in a high robbery area, (2) observed the subject standing on the sidewalk and looking into a store, (3) businesses were about to close, (4) and the subject remained in the same spot for 15 minutes—it was not a bus stop, the officer performed a stop on the subject to investigate whether or not a robbery was in motion. During the stop, because (1) robberies involve dangerous weapons and robbers are dangerous and (2) the subject was verbally combative—yelling, "you are harassing me," the officer performed a pat-down.[125]

In the above example, notice how the officer explained the reason for the stop by listing factors. And notice how the officer explained the reason for the frisk by listing factors.

> Example 6.6: The officer performed a stop on the subject because, while (1) patrolling in a heavy narcotics neighborhood, the subject, who was standing still, (2) took flight upon the officer's presence in the area. The officer wanted to make sure that the subject was not involved in criminal activity.[126] Because the subject was (1) evasive—he ran, (2) was in a heavy narcotics neighborhood—from the officer's experience, narcotics usually involve firearms, and was (3) verbally combative—yelling "you have no right to stop me!," the officer performed a frisk.

In the above example, notice that the same factors that justified the stop can be used to justify the frisk. Again, notice that two explanations are required: one for the stop and one for the frisk.

> Example 6.7: After a traffic stop for a red light infraction, the officer performed a frisk on the driver because (1) the driver was verbally combative—yelling "Why are you stopping me?," (2) the area was known for shootings—2 people were killed yesterday, and (3) the driver was not following the officer's order to remain inside the car.

---

[125] See *Terry,* 392 U.S. at 29-30 (The Supreme Court stated that it is reasonable to infer that a suspected robber is armed and dangerous because a robbery implies that weapons are present.).

[126] See *Illinois v. Wardlow,* 528 U.S. 119 (2000) (The Supreme Court stated that a person running upon the presence of the police is not enough to perform a stop on the person who ran. But the Supreme Court made it clear that if the person runs upon the presence of the police and it is in a heavy narcotics neighborhood, then the two factors are enough to perform a stop on the person who ran.).

In the above example, notice that the officer gave three factors for the frisk. This is what it means to have reasonable articulable suspicion that the subject is armed and presently dangerous. The point is that a pat-down does not follow automatically from a stop. The legal justification for the frisk is that the officer has reasonable articulable suspicion that the subject is armed and presently dangerous. If the weapon is lawfully possessed, then the officer returns the weapon at the completion of the investigation. If it is an illegal weapon, then the officer arrests the subject for carrying the illegal weapon.

Some states have put the authority to perform a frisk into a statute. For example, Illinois enacted 725 ILCS 5/108-1.01.

> **When a peace officer has stopped a person for temporary questioning pursuant to Section 107-14 of this Code and reasonably suspects that he or another is in danger of attack, he may search the person for weapons. If the officer discovers a weapon, he may take it until the completion of the questioning, at which time he shall either return the weapon, if lawfully possessed, or arrest the person so questioned.**[127]

In short, the officer has to explain why the frisk was performed.

Explaining the Reason for the Frisk

Some crimes infer that a weapon is involved thus justifying a frisk.[128] A bulge in the clothing is a factor that will strengthen the officer's belief that the subject is armed and dangerous.[129] Other factors that support an officer's belief that the subject is armed and dangerous are (1) the subject appears to be under the influence of drugs,[130] (2) it is a heavy narcotics area,[131] (3) the hour is late, [132] and (4) a face-to-face complainant alleges that the subject has a firearm.[133] The police officer should list all the factors that were present when he or she performed the frisk.

---

[127] See 725 ILCS 5/108-1.01 (quoting Laws 1968, p. 218) (The boldface was added by the author.).
[128] *Terry*, 392 U.S. at 28.
[129] *Pennsylvania v. Mimms*, 434 U.S. 106, 111-112 (1977).
[130] *Michigan v. Long*, 463 U.S. 1032, 1150 (1983).
[131] *Illinois v. Wardlow*, 528 U.S. at 124.
[132] *Mimms*, 434 U.S. at 1150.
[133] *Adams*, 407 U.S. at 147 (The Supreme Court ruled that information from a face-to-face complainant can be used as a factor for a stop and a frisk.).

Diagram 6.3

THE LEVELS OF PROOF FOR EVIDENCE GATHERING

A SEARCH GOVERNED BY THE FOURTH AMDENDMENT

- NEED PROBABLE CAUSE
- IF NO EXCEPTION APPLIES, THEN NEED A WARRANT

THE *TERRY* FRISK (THE PROTECTIVE PAT-DOWN)

- NEED REASONABLE SUSPICION THAT THE SUBJECT IS PRESENTLY "ARMED AND DANGEROUS"

THE CARETAKER ENCOUNTER

- A PERSON'S WELFARE IS A CONCERN
- THE PROTECTION OF PROPERTY IS A CONCERN

PLAIN VIEW

- THE OFFICER HAS A LEGAL RIGHT TO BE PRESENT
- THE OFFICER CAN READILY GRAB THE OBJECT
- THE ILLEGALITY OF THE OBJECT IS OBVIOUS

Examples of Factors for a Frisk

- THE SUSPECTED CRIME IMPLIES A WEAPON
- A BULGE IN THE SUSPECT'S CLOTHING
- THE SUSPECT APPEARS TO BE UNDER THE INFLUENCE OF DRUGS
- IT IS A HEAVY NARCOTICS AREA, DRUGS AND FIREARMS GO TOGETHER
- THE HOUR IS LATE
- A FACE-TO-FACE COMPLAINANT ALLLEGES THAT THE SUBJECT HAS A FIREARM

The Plain Feel Law (Doctrine)

Related to the frisk, the plain feel doctrine allows police officers to rely on their sense of touch while conducting a pat-down for weapons. If, while performing a pat-down for weapons, the officer feels something that is immediately apparent to be contraband, then the officer can retrieve the item; if the item is contraband, then the officer may arrest the subject. For example, while performing a frisk, if the officer feels a lump that the officer immediately recognizes as crack cocaine, then the officer is allowed to remove the lump from the clothing. Squeezing, sliding, or other manipulation of the object is not allowed. Additionally, the officer's training and experience play a role. The training and experience of the officer play a major role in proving that the officer knows what the contraband feels like.[134] So, the officer uses his or her sense of touch to detect drugs while performing a frisk for weapons. (The frisk has to be supported by reasonable articulable suspicion; and this is done by stating the factors that led the officer to believe that the subject was presently armed and dangerous.)

[134] *Minnesota v. Dickerson,* 508 U.S. 366 (1993).

Katz v. United States (1967)[135]

Once inside an enclosed telephone booth, Katz placed a call and transmitted wagering information from Los Angeles to Miami. Despite not having a warrant, FBI agents, prior to Katz's call, had connected a recording and listening device to the telephonic wire outside of the phone booth. The transmission of the wagering information over a telephone line was a violation of a federal statute. Katz was convicted of the illegal act (transmitting wagering information over a telephone line); and the court of appeals affirmed the conviction. (This means that, at this point, Katz is guilty.) The case, thereafter, reached the Supreme Court of the United States ("the Supreme Court").

The Supreme Court had to decide whether the listening to Katz's conversation and the recording of the same were a violation of the Fourth Amendment because they were done without a warrant. The Supreme Court reasoned that, even though there was no physical intrusion into the phone booth, Katz was entitled to privacy. Additionally, The Supreme Court announced a two part test: (1) the person must subjectively expect privacy—this means that the person is looking for privacy—and (2) the expectation of privacy must be reasonable; in other words the expectation of privacy is one that society is willing to recognize as reasonable.

Based on this, the court said that the FBI's tapping of the phone violated Katz's Fourth Amendment rights. The court reached this conclusion by reasoning that Katz used an enclosed phone booth—he shut the door—because he expected privacy. (This is part one of the test.) Additionally, the court stated that a person is entitled to expect privacy inside a phone booth. (This is the second part of the test—expecting privacy inside a phone booth is reasonable.) Based on this, the court concluded that, because the FBI agents did not have a warrant, the tapping of the telephone was a violation of the Fourth Amendment. This means that the recording of the conversation and evidence obtained from the same could not be used against Katz.

[135] *Katz v. United States,* 389 U.S. 347 (1967).

Katz v. United States (1967)

In summary, tapping a phone line, despite the lack of a physical intrusion into the premises, is a search. In the *Katz* case the court stated that a warrant was required. Additionally, because the FBI agents did not have a warrant, the evidence obtained from tapping the telephone was inadmissible. Since the evidence could not be used, Katz conviction was overturned.

The general rule is that unless an exception to the warrant requirement applies and there is time to get a warrant then the police officer should secure a warrant. So, if time and circumstances permit, then get a warrant. If a warrant is not obtained, then the burden of showing why it was not feasible to get a warrant falls on the police officers and prosecutors. Additionally, if the situation satisfies the *Katz* two part test, then a warrant is probably required.

> (1) The person must subjectively expect privacy—this means that the person is looking for privacy.
>
> (2) And the expectation of privacy must be reasonable; in other words the expectation of privacy is one that society is willing to recognize as reasonable.[136]

Again, search warrants are preferred. There are times when it is not practical to get a search warrant. So, the exceptions to the search warrant requirement will be discussed later.

Also, except for a few exceptions, a search warrant is required for searching someone's home. (The exceptions will be discussed later.) Furthermore, there is an automobile exception.

If a police officer has probable cause (enough factors) to believe that there is contraband in an automobile that is in motion, then the police officer can stop the car and search it without a warrant.[137] Remember that seizures (stops) do not require probable cause—just reasonable articulable suspicion of criminal activity. (This is a lower standard than probable cause.)

---

[136] *Katz*, 389 U.S. at 361.

[137] *Carroll v. United States*, 267 U.S. 132 (1925) (This case created the automobile exception. Also, this case gives a good explanation of probable cause.).

Florida v. Bostick[139]

Two Broward County Sherriff's Department Officers boarded a Greyhound bus on which Bostick was a passenger. And, without articulable suspicion that Bostick was involved in criminal activity, the officers asked Bostick for permission to search his luggage; the officers advised Bostick of his right to refuse. Bostick consented to the search.

After the officers found cocaine in Bostick's luggage, Bostick was arrested for drug trafficking. Bostick argued that the cocaine should be suppressed because it was seized in violation of his Fourth Amendment rights. (Bostick claimed that he was seized because the police officers towered over him when he was sitting down on the bus and he had very little space to move around.) The trial court denied Bostick's request to suppress the evidence. The Florida Court of Appeals affirmed the trial court's decision. And the State Supreme Court ruled that the practice of "working the buses" (officers boarding buses and asking for permission to search the passengers' luggage) was unconstitutional. Thereafter, the case reached the Supreme Court of the United States ("the Supreme Court").

The question before the Supreme Court was whether a police encounter on a bus automatically amounted to a seizure (this is how the Supreme Court framed the question). The Supreme Court stated that just because a police officer approaches a person does not mean that the person is seized. Moreover, The Supreme Court explained that, despite the fact that a person would not want to get off the bus for fear of being stranded, the location of the encounter—the bus—was only one factor in determining whether the person had being seized.

The Supreme Court explained that the totality of the circumstances is considered when deciding whether a person has being seized. Moreover, the court reasoned that the officers, in this case, did not have their firearms drawn. Additionally, the officers advised Bostick of his right to refuse. Furthermore, the Supreme Court noted that Bostick would not have felt free to leave even if the officers were not present—because, according to The Supreme Court, Bostick wanted to stay on the bus.

[139] *Florida v. Bostick,* 501 U.S. 429 (1991).

United States v. Mendenhall[140]

The Issue before the Supreme Court of the United States was whether the respondent (the arrestee) had validly consented to a corporal search (a body search) and to a police encounter. The respondent argued that the search and seizure were unconstitutional, under the Fourth Amendment. If the search and seizure were unconstitutional then the evidence, cocaine, would have been excluded from evidence and Mendenhall's conviction would have been overturned.

Federal Agents approached the respondent after they observed behavior, which they believed to be characteristics of persons illegally carrying unlawful drugs. The Agents testified that Sylvia Mendenhall was the last person to get off the plane. Additionally, the agents stated that Mendenhall would scan the area before proceeding farther. In sum, this got the attention of the agents, who were working in an airport.

Consequently, due to the suspicion, the agents approached Mendenhall and asked to see Mendenhall's identification and plane ticket. Mendenhall gave the agents her driver's license and her airplane ticket. The agents noticed that the airplane ticket was purchased under a different name "Anette Ford." (The documents were returned to Mendenhall.) Thereafter, the agents asked Mendenhall to accompany the agents to the DEA office located in the airport. The officer was 50 feet away from the initial encounter.

While at the office, one of the agents asked Mendenhall if she would allow a search of her person and handbag. Additionally, Mendenhall was advised that she could decline the request. Mendenhall consented to the search. After the consent, a female police officer was summoned to conduct the search. The female officer asked Mendenhall if she consented to the search. Mendenhall replied that she had consented to the search. Mendenhall was asked to remove her clothing. While disrobing, Mendenhall took from her undergarments two small bags, one which contained cocaine.

In conclusion, the Supreme Court ruled that the encounter was consensual and that the consent to search was voluntarily given.

[140] *United States v. Mendenhall,* 446 U.S. 544 (1980).

Review of Police/Citizen Encounters

As mentioned before, police officers are allowed to approach people who are on the public way and start a conversation. The officers are allowed to ask questions. As long as a reasonable person in the same situation would feel free to leave, the encounter is not a seizure. This means that, despite the absence of reasonable suspicion, an officer may legally approach people who are standing on the sidewalk and ask questions (or just have a conversation). There are factors that might turn the encounter into a seizure (a stop). (Recall that reasonable suspicion of a crime is required for a stop.) Some of these factors will be discussed shortly.

To review, a seizure requires reasonable suspicion (or probable cause for an arrest). Reasonable suspicion means that the police officer is able to articulate facts that led the officer to believe that a crime was about to be committed, was being committed, or had being committed. These facts have to amount to more than a hunch. How many facts are needed to legally justify a seizure? There is no set rule. The officer should articulate all the facts that are available.

Moreover, related to the stop, recall that the frisk (pat down for weapons) requires additional facts that made the officer believe that the suspect was armed and presently dangerous. To elaborate, just because the stop is justified does not mean that the frisk is justified.

In sum, the types of police/citizen encounters where discussed in detail in prior chapters. The remainder of this chapter focuses on factors that make a police/citizen encounter a seizure (a stop). The cases that follow are a few of the major cases that have defined the meaning of a seizure. Moreover, the cases have clarified a few of the officer's legal authority during vehicular stops.

City of Chicago v. Morales[141]

Due to the troubles that the street gangs in Chicago were causing, (increased murder rate, intimidating law-abiding citizens, and fights), the Chicago City Council enacted the "Gang Congregation Ordinance." This law prohibited gang members from congregating with any other persons. In other words, if at least one street gang member was standing on the public way with at least one more person (the other person did not have to be a street gang member), then it was against the law. The Chicago statute made it a crime (if at least one person was a street gang member) to loiter in one spot. Additionally, the law defined loitering as to stand in one place with no apparent purpose.

Shortly after the gang loitering law was created, the Chicago Police Department enacted a rule that ordered police officers to disperse people who were in violation of the gang loitering law. Furthermore, if the people refused to walk away, then the officer would proceed to arrest the person(s) who refused to go away. An Illinois trial court held that the ordinance was unconstitutional because it was too vague. It was too vague because it failed to notify people of exactly what type of conduct was illegal.

The Supreme Court acknowledged that street gangs are a big problem. As far as the gang loitering statute, the Supreme Court stated that the law gave police officers too much discretion on whom to enforce the law and arrest. Additionally, the Supreme Court mentioned that the law did not provide enough notice to the citizens of what type of conduct was prohibited.

In short, the street loitering law was struck down because it violated the Due Process Clause of the Fourteenth Amendment to the Federal Constitution; the law was void for vagueness. The two major reasons that the law violated the Fourteenth Amendment were that (1) the law gave the police officer too much discretion in deciding whom to disperse (the officer decided who was engaged in gang loitering and therefore subject to dispersal) and (2) the statute did not provide enough guidance to the citizens (the phrase "with no apparent purpose" was too vague to put the citizens on notice of what acts were prohibited).

[141] *City of Chicago v. Morales,* 527 U.S. 41 (1999).

In What Situation Is a Person Stopped (Seized)?

The Supreme Court, in *Mendenhall*, gave the test to use to determine whether a person has been seized.

> We conclude that a person has been "seized" within the meaning of the Fourth Amendment only if, in view of all of the circumstances surrounding the incident, a reasonable person would have believed that he was not free to leave.[142]

This means that not all encounters between police officers and citizens are seizures. In addition, even if a person feels that he or she has been seized, it might not be a seizure because a reasonable person in the same situation would not have felt that he or she was not free to go. For example, in *Chesternut*, the defendant argued that he was seized when a patrol car drove alongside of him. In addition, the Supreme Court ruled that a reasonable person, in the same situation, would not feel seized.[143] Additionally, the Supreme Court, in *Mendenhall*, gave some of the factors that might make an encounter a seizure:

1. the threatening presence of several officers,
2. the display of a weapon by an officer,
3. physical touching,
4. tone of voice or language indicating that the citizen must comply,
5. the location of the encounter,
6. ordering the citizen to move to a certain spot, and
7. an officer's demand to see identification.[144]

These are the factors from the *Mendenhall* case. It is not a complete list. Moreover, by applying the factors to the facts in *Chesternut*, Chesternut was not seized. There was no physical touching. Chesternut was free to move. The officer did not order Chesternut to stop. The officer did not demand to see identification. The officer did not display a weapon.

The cases that follow explain when a police encounter is a seizure. (Remember that reasonable articulable suspicion is needed for a seizure.)

---

[142] *Id.* at 544.

[143] *Michigan v. Chesternut,* 486 U.S. 567 (1988) (Chesternut was not seized because an officer was driving by his side.).

[144] *Mendenhall,* 446 U.S. at 544-545.

Florida v. Royer[145]

Traveling under an assumed name (not the real name), with two suitcases, Royer was approached by two detectives who asked if Royer had a moment to talk. Royer answered in the affirmative. Thereafter, the detectives asked Royer for his identification and his airline ticket. Royer gave the detectives the two documents. The detectives asked Royer about the different name—Holt—that was on airline ticket. Royer stated that a friend had obtained the ticket for Royer.

Without returning Royer's documents, the detectives informed Royer that they had reason to believe that Royer was involved in drug trafficking; the detectives asked Royer to go with them to a room. Without permission, one of the detectives grabbed Royer's luggage. While in the room, without verbally consenting, after a detective's request, Royer produced a key and opened one of the suitcases; the suitcase contained marijuana.

Royer stated that he did not know the combination to the second suitcase; Royer did not object to the suitcase being pried open. After forcing the second suitcase open and finding more marijuana, the detectives arrested Royer for felony possession of marijuana. The case reached the Supreme Court.

The Supreme Court reasoned that Royer's detention (the confinement in a room) had exceeded the scope of a permissible investigatory stop. The Supreme Court stated that Royer was illegally detained and that any consent to the opening of Royer's suitcases was therefore invalid; probable cause was required.

In short, the Supreme Court stated that Royer's consent to the opening of the suitcases was no good because the consent was tarnished by the illegal detention. (This case is very similar to other Supreme Court cases. The one difference in this case, that might have turned the police encounter into a seizure—as opposed to a voluntary encounter, is the fact that the detectives kept Royer's identification and flight ticket.) An important aspect of this case is that confining someone in a room might exceed the scope of an investigatory detention.

[145] *Florida v. Royer,* 460 U.S. 491 (1983) (notice the resemblance to the *Mendenhall* case).

California v. Hodari (1991)[146]

An Oakland California police officer, Pertoso, was patrolling a high crime neighborhood in an unmarked police car. As Pertoso was turning a corner, he noticed a group of people huddled together. The people in the group noticed the unmarked police car; and they took flight. Pertoso, who was wearing street clothes with a jacket bearing the word "Police" on the front, got out of his car and gave chase. Pertoso focused on Hodari—one of the persons who fled upon seeing the unmarked police car.

Before Pertoso tackled Hodari, Hodari tossed crack cocaine in the form of a rock. After Pertoso tackled and secured Hodari, Pertoso recovered the rock and radioed for assistance. Hodari moved to have the evidence suppressed by arguing that the rock had been obtained by an unlawful seizure.

The trial court denied Hodari's request. But the State Court of Appeal agreed with Hodari and reversed the trial court. This means that the State Court of Appeals agreed that Hodari was seized when Perstoso chased Hodari.

Subsequently, due to the dispute about the seizure, the case reached the Supreme Court of the United States ("the Supreme Court"). So, the question before the Supreme Court was whether Hodari was seized when Pertoso began running towards Hodari. This was crucial because if Hodari was seized when Perstoso started the chase, then the crack cocaine would not have been admissible. (There was no reasonable suspicion for a seizure.)

In summary, the Supreme Court ruled that, because Hodari decided to run—thereby, not submitting to the show of force, there was no seizure during the foot chase. Additionally, the Supreme Court ruled that the seizure occurred when Pertoso physically tackled Hodari. Before the tackling, however, Hodari had already discarded the cocaine. This means that, according to the Supreme Court's reasoning, the cocaine was legally obtained. The end result of this is that the cocaine was used as evidence against Hodari because it was lawfully obtained. The cocaine was recovered before Hodari was seized.

[146] *California v. Hodari,* 499 U.S. 621 (1991).

Diagram 6.4

THE THREE STEP PROCESS FOR EXPLAINING A REASONABLE STOP

ONE

- **APPLY THE TOTALITY OF THE CIRCUMSTANCES**

TWO

- **LIST ALL THE FACTORS**

THREE

- **EXPLAIN AT LEAST ONE FACTOR THAT LINKS THE SUBJECT TO THE SUSPICIOUS ACTIVITY**

Stopping Vehicles

Traffic stops are treated like *Terry* stops. The driver who is pulled over for a traffic infraction or an investigatory detention (based on reasonable articulable suspicion) is not under a custodial arrest.[147] A passenger can be the suspicious person, also. So, an officer may ask a moderate number of questions to confirm or dispel the officer's suspicions.[148] (In some states, due to identification statutes, the legally seized person is required to supply basic identification information.)[149] The driver or passenger is not obligated to answer the questions.[150] But if the suspect's answers provide the officer with probable cause to arrest, then the officer may arrest the suspect.[151]

Like a Terry stop, the officer is still allowed to perform a protective frisk of the driver or passenger based on reasonable articulable suspicion that the person is armed and presently dangerous. Additionally, the protective frisk extends to the vehicle—all areas that are accessible from the passenger compartment.[152] The cases that follow provide more insight on the officer's authority during investigatory stops.

United States v. Sharpe[153]

While patrolling an area known for narcotics trafficking, a Drug Enforcement Administration (DEA) agent noticed a pickup truck equipped with a camper shell that appeared to be overloaded; the truck was fairly close to the ground. While following the truck, the DEA agent noticed that the truck did neither sway nor bounce around curves. Additionally, there was a blue Pontiac travelling in conjunction with the truck. Consequently, the DEA agent decided to make an investigative stop.

---

[147] *Berkemer v. Carty,* 468 U.S. 420, 439-440 (1984).

[148] *Id.* at 439.

[149] See *Hiibel v. Nevada,* 542 U.S. 177 (2004)(The Supreme Court ruled that these statutes are lawful; a legal seizure is required); Illinois has such a statute, 720 ILCS 5/31-4.5.

[150] *Id.*

[151] *Id.*

[152] *Michigan v. Long,* 463 U.S. 1032 (1983).

[153] *United States v. Sharpe,* 470 U.S. 675 (1985).

United States v. Sharpe

Before the DEA agent, Cooke, made the stop, Cooke radioed for assistance. Officer Thrasher answered the call. Cooke pulled the Pontiac over; and farther down the road, Thrasher pulled the truck over and ordered the driver, Savage, to get out. Thrasher detained Savage. Moreover, Cooke joined Thrasher around 15 minutes later. Cook stepped on the back of the truck and it did not go any lower. This confirmed Cooke's suspicion that the truck was overloaded. Thereafter, Cook pressed his nose against the rear glass of the truck; Cooke smelled marijuana.

Cook opened the rear of the truck and he noticed several packages. Cook had seen similar packages before that contained marijuana. Consequently, the driver of the Pontiac, Davis, and Savage were arrested. A total of 43 packages of marijuana, weighing 2,629 pounds, were recovered. The arrestees were convicted.

The appeals court reversed the conviction because the investigative stop, which lasted about 20 minutes, was unlawful because it was too long, according to the court. Thereafter, the case reached the Supreme Court of the United States ("the Supreme Court"). The question before the court was whether the investigative stop was lawful.

The Supreme Court addressed this concern in two parts. First, as to part one—whether the stop was justified, The Supreme Court held that the stop was supported by reasonable articulable suspicion. The second part of the inquiry was whether the stop was unconstitutional because it lasted for 20 minutes.

The Supreme Court stated that there are no strict time limitations on investigatory stops. The Supreme Court stressed that the test was whether the officer pursued the investigation in a diligent manner. Put another way, this means that an investigatory stop does not have a predefined time limit. Based on this, The Supreme Court held that the stop was lawful because Cook diligently pursued the investigation.

In conclusion, this case holds that an investigative stop does not have a predefined time limit. If the officer is acting diligently to confirm or dispel his or her suspicions, then a 30-minute detention might very well be reasonable. In this case, The Supreme Court held that a 20-minute investigative stop was lawful. Therefore, based on this case, there is no predetermined time limit on an investigatory stop.

Pennsylvania v. Mimms[154]

Mimms, the respondent, was pulled over because he was observed driving a vehicle with an expired plate. During the seizure, Mimms was asked by one of the two officers who pulled Mimms over to step out of the vehicle. As Mimms exited the car, the officer noticed a large bulge on Mimms's jacket.

Fearing that the bulge might be a weapon, the officer performed a pat-down (frisk) and recovered a loaded .38 caliber revolver. Thereafter, the officer recovered a .32 caliber revolver from the other passenger in Mimms's car. Mimms was arrested for carrying a concealed deadly weapon and for carrying a firearm without a license. Mimms was convicted on both counts at the trial level. The Supreme Court of Pennsylvania reversed the conviction. (This means that, at this point, Mimms is not guilty.) Thereafter, the Supreme Court of the United States was asked to review the case.

The Supreme Court of the United States was asked to answer the question whether the officer violated Mimms's Fourth Amendment right by requiring Mimms to get out of his car. (Put another way, does a police officer have the authority, without articulable suspicion to support the increased Fourth Amendment intrusion, to order the driver to get out of the car.) (For the constitutional scholars, it is the Fourteenth Amendment that is at issue because the Philadelphia police officers were not federal agents—but the result is the same.) It is important to note that removing drivers from their cars was common practice among Philadelphia police officers. The Philadelphia police officers did this for safety. This allowed the officers to watch the driver's movements.

Related to safety, the Supreme Court of the United States noted that traffic stops are dangerous because officers are shot and killed during traffic stops. Additionally, the court stated that it is dangerous for an officer to stand in the middle of the street. (There is the risk of the officer being hit by a passing automobile.) This means that, on the one hand, the court weighed—considered—the safety of the officer.

[154] *Pennsylvanis v. Mimms,* 434 U.S. 106 (1997).

Pennsylvania v. Mimms

On the other hand, the court considered the intrusion on the driver by requiring the driver to step out of the vehicle. The court agreed that to have the driver step out of the car is an intrusion. However, the court said that it was a small intrusion against the competing interest of the safety of the officer.

In summary, the court concluded that, due to the risk to the safety of the officer, a police officer is allowed as a matter of course (this means that the officer does not have to explain or justify himself or herself) to order the driver to get out of the vehicle. In other words, the officer does not need further suspicion of wrongdoing (or that the driver is armed and dangerous) to order the driver to step out of the vehicle. It is important to note that the ordering the driver out of the car is an automatic right of the officer; but the pat-down for weapons is a separate step. The pat-down for weapons has to be articulated and justified by reasonable suspicion that the driver is armed and dangerous (*Terry v. Ohio*). In this case, the officer testified that he performed a frisk because he observed a large bulge and he feared that the bulge might be a weapon.

Maryland v. Wilson[155]

A Maryland state trooper observed a car traveling at a speed of 64 miles per hour in a 55 mile per hour zone. Consequently, the state trooper activated his lights and sirens and signaled the car to pull over. Despite the trooper's attempt to pull the car over, the car continued driving for another mile and a half. During this trip, the trooper noticed that there were three occupants in the car. Additionally, the trooper noticed that the two passengers looked in his direction and ducked from view a few times. Eventually, the car stopped.

[155] *Maryland v. Wilson,* 519 U.S. 408 (1997).

Maryland v. Wilson

During the stop, the state trooper noticed that the passenger, Wilson, in the front seat was sweating and appeared extremely nervous. Thereafter, the trooper ordered Wilson to get out of the car. As Wilson got out the vehicle, some crack cocaine fell to the ground; so, Wilson was arrested and charged with possession of cocaine with intent to distribute. Wilson argued that the trooper's ordering him out of the car constituted and unreasonable seizure.

The trial court agreed with Wilson and ordered that the evidence be suppressed. (This means that if the evidence is suppressed, then Wilson will not get convicted.) Thereafter, the appellate court agreed with the trial court. (At this point, Wilson cannot get convicted because the crack cocaine is not admissible as evidence because it was discovered during an "unreasonable seizure.") Eventually, the case made it to the Supreme Court of the United States.

So, the Supreme Court had to decide whether an officer had the right to order a passenger to get out of the car. (This is different from *Pennsylvania v. Mimms*, where The Supreme Court—in 1977—ruled that an officer, without reasonable articulable suspicion, during a lawful traffic stop, has the absolute right to order the driver to get out of the car.) The Supreme Court reasoned that the applicable standard in deciding this Fourth Amendment intrusion is reasonableness based on the totality of the circumstances.

In deciding the question of whether the state trooper acted reasonably in ordering Wilson to get out of the car, the Supreme Court considered that many officers are killed during traffic stops. Additionally, the court considered that getting the passengers out of the car was a reasonable intrusion when compared to the concern of the safety of police officers. The court ruled that police officers have the authority, without reasonable articulable suspicion of danger to the officer or of criminal activity, to order the passengers to get out of the vehicle.

In conclusion, police officers have the absolute right (without having to articulate or justify themselves) to order the passengers to get out of the car. This case is significant because it gives police officers the complete authority to order the passengers to get out of the car. So, together with prior case law, police officers have the absolute right to order the driver and all passengers to get out of the car.

Brendlin v. California[156]

Police officers stopped a car to check its registration. The police officers had neither reasonable articulable suspicion nor probable cause to detain the car. During the seizure, one of the officers recognized Brendlin as a parole violator. The officer returned to his police vehicle where he checked whether Brendlin was a parole violator. Through the police radio, the police officers learned that there was an arrest warrant (for violation of parole) for Brendlin.

Armed with this information, the officers proceeded to arrest Brendlin; a search of the Brendlin's person, the car, and the driver followed. The officers recovered an orange syringe cap from Brendlin's person. Syringes and a plastic bag containing cannabis were recovered from the driver's person. Tubing, a scale, and other items used in the manufacture of methamphetamine were found in the car. Consequently, Brendlin was charged with possessing drugs and the manufacture of methamphetamine.

Brendlin asked the court to suppress the evidence because the items were found during an illegal search and seizure. Brendlin argued that the police had neither probable cause nor reasonable suspicion to stop the car. So, the search and seizure was a violation of Brendlin's Fourth Amendment right, Brendlin argued. The state of California agreed that the officers had neither probable cause nor reasonable suspicion to stop the car.

However, the state of California argued that Brendlin was not seized (because the seizure was focused on the driver of the car) and therefore was not entitled to the protections of the Fourth Amendment. (For the constitutional scholars, the applicable Constitutional Amendment is the Fourteenth but the end result is the same.) So, the Supreme Court of the United States had to answer the question of whether a passenger in a car is seized when police officers stop a vehicle

The Supreme Court reasoned that because (applying the reasonable person standard) a passenger in a vehicle would feel seized (not free to leave) when police officers stop the vehicle, passengers are seized. Consequently, because passengers are seized, they are entitled to the protections of the Fourth Amendment.

---

[156] *Brendlin v. California,* 551 U.S. 249 (2007).

Brendlin v. California

This case is important because, before it was decided, it was not too clear whether, during a lawful traffic stop, the passengers were seized. Now it is clear that the passengers are seized and that police officers have the authority to detain everybody that is inside the vehicle.

In summary, the court said that police officers are in full control of their traffic stops. (The court considered issues related to officer safety—it is not safe to have people moving around during the investigation). Again, during a lawful traffic stop, (this is the significance of this case), police officers are allowed to exercise control over every person inside that car; and, at the same time, everyone inside the car, is entitled to the protections of the Fourth Amendment, during a lawful traffic stop.

Traffic Stops and the Officer's Authority

During a lawful traffic stop, a police officer has the authority to perform certain actions. These are a few of the police officer's rights:

1. order the driver out of the car (no justification needed),[157]
2. order all the passengers out of the car (no justification needed),[158]
3. seize every occupant of the vehicle (no justification needed),[159] and
4. frisk the areas of the vehicle that are immediately accessible to the occupants for weapons (one justified frisk is required, see diagram 6.5).[160]

During the frisk of the vehicle (also called a pat-down of a car), the officer may search the areas of the vehicle that are (1) accessible from the passenger compartment and (2) are large enough to contain a weapon.[161] (One justified frisk of an occupant of the car is required; in other words, a justified frisk of one of the occupants allows the officer to frisk the car without further explanation.)

---

[157] *Mimms,* 433 U.S.
[158] *Wilson,* 519 U.S.
[159] *Brendlin,* 551 U.S.
[160] *Long,* 463 U.S.
[161] *Id.*

Diagram 6.5

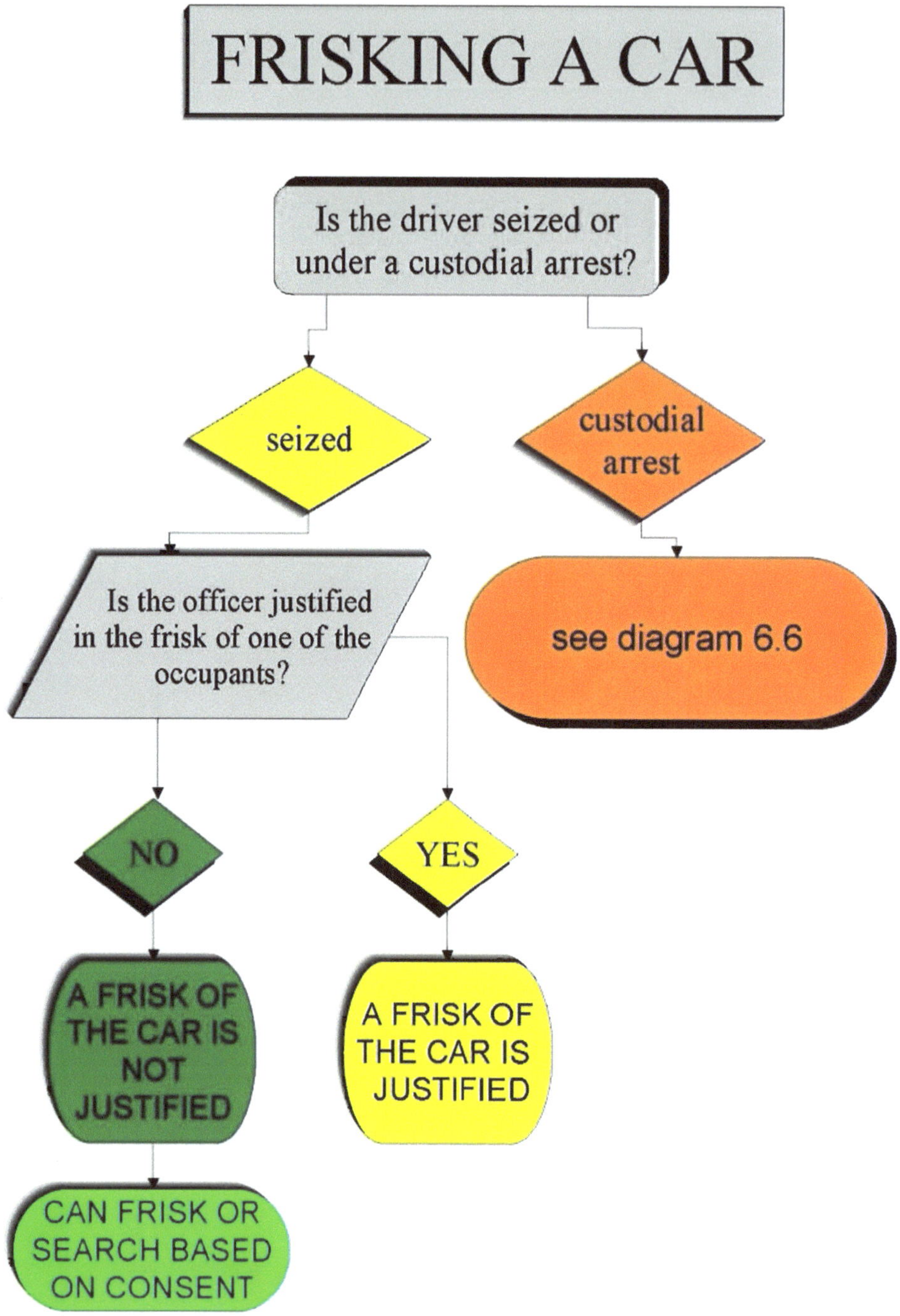
FRISKING A CAR
Is the driver seized or under a custodial arrest?
seized
custodial arrest
Is the officer justified in the frisk of one of the occupants?
see diagram 6.6
NO
YES
A FRISK OF THE CAR IS NOT JUSTIFIED
A FRISK OF THE CAR IS JUSTIFIED
CAN FRISK OR SEARCH BASED ON CONSENT

Diagram 6.6

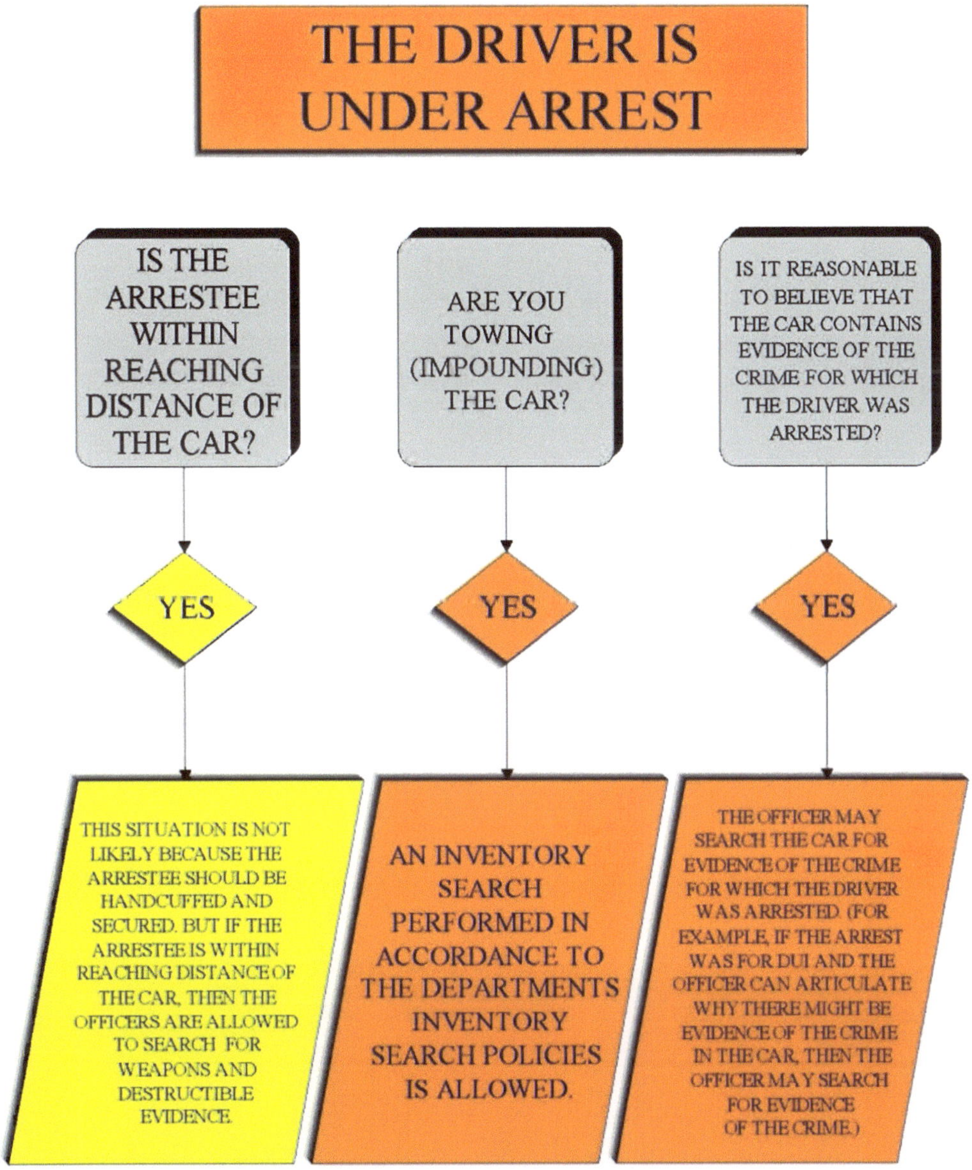
THE DRIVER IS UNDER ARREST
IS THE ARRESTEE WITHIN REACHING DISTANCE OF THE CAR?
ARE YOU TOWING (IMPOUNDING) THE CAR?
IS IT REASONABLE TO BELIEVE THAT THE CAR CONTAINS EVIDENCE OF THE CRIME FOR WHICH THE DRIVER WAS ARRESTED?
YES
YES
YES
THIS SITUATION IS NOT LIKELY BECAUSE THE ARRESTEE SHOULD BE HANDCUFFED AND SECURED. BUT IF THE ARRESTEE IS WITHIN REACHING DISTANCE OF THE CAR, THEN THE OFFICERS ARE ALLOWED TO SEARCH FOR WEAPONS AND DESTRUCTIBLE EVIDENCE.
AN INVENTORY SEARCH PERFORMED IN ACCORDANCE TO THE DEPARTMENTS INVENTORY SEARCH POLICIES IS ALLOWED.
THE OFFICER MAY SEARCH THE CAR FOR EVIDENCE OF THE CRIME FOR WHICH THE DRIVER WAS ARRESTED. (FOR EXAMPLE, IF THE ARREST WAS FOR DUI AND THE OFFICER CAN ARTICULATE WHY THERE MIGHT BE EVIDENCE OF THE CRIME IN THE CAR, THEN THE OFFICER MAY SEARCH FOR EVIDENCE OF THE CRIME.)

Review

Objectives:

1. Recognize when a stop is authorized.

- The stop is also known as the *Terry* stop.[162] A stop is a seizure and the subject is not free to leave. This type of police/citizen encounter requires reasonable articulable suspicion that criminal activity is afoot.[163] Put another way, the police officer has to explain why the stop was made.

2. Recognize when a frisk is authorized.

- During the stop, if the police officer has reasonable articulable suspicion that the subject is "presently armed and dangerous," then the police officer may legally perform a frisk—a limited search for weapons.[164]

[162] *Terry v. Ohio*, 392 U.S. 1 (1969) (This case created the investigatory detention—the stop—for police officers; prior to this case, without probable cause, a police officer could not legally seize a person.) *Brinegar*, 338 U.S. at 178-179 (In 1948, the concurring judge, Justice Burton, argued that police officers should be allowed to conduct investigatory stops; it took nineteen years for the investigatory stop to materialize.).

[163] *Terry*, 392 U.S. at 29-30 (The Supreme Court stated that, because the officer had reasonable articulable suspicion that a robbery was about to be committed, both the seizure and the frisk were reasonable and legal.).

[164] *Id.*

3. Understand the "Plain Feel" law.

- The plain feel doctrine allows police officers to rely on their sense of touch while conducting a pat-down for weapons. If, while performing a pat-down for weapons, the officer feels something that is immediately apparent to be contraband, then the officer can retrieve the item; if the item is contraband, then the officer may arrest the subject. For example, while performing a frisk, if the officer feels a lump that the officer immediately recognizes as crack cocaine, then the officer remove the lump from the clothing. Squeezing, sliding, or other manipulation of the object is not allowed. Additionally, the officer's training and experience play a role. The training and experience of the officer play a major role in proving that the officer knows what the contraband feels like.[165]

4. Recognize when a search warrant is required.

- The general rule is that unless an exception to the warrant requirement applies and there is time to get a warrant then the police officer should secure a warrant. So, if time and circumstances permit, then get a warrant. If a warrant is not obtained, then the burden of showing why it was not feasible to get a warrant falls on the police officers and prosecutors. Additionally, if the situation satisfies the *Katz* two part test, then a warrant is probably required.
    - (1) The person must subjectively expect privacy—this means that the person is looking for privacy.
    - (2) And the expectation of privacy must be reasonable; in other words the expectation of privacy is one that society is willing to recognize as reasonable.[166]

[165] *Minnesota v. Dickerson,* 508 U.S. 366 (1993).
[166] *Katz,* 389 U.S. at 361.

Conclusion

It is important to remember that a stop requires a legal justification—an explanation of why the person was stopped. Additionally, the frisk does not follow automatically from the stop. In other words, a frisk is not justified just because the stop is justified. (There are situations where the factors that justified the stop will justify the frisk—*Terry v. Ohio*; but the officer still needs to explain that the factors for the stop justified the frisk. For example, while investigating a possible robbery, it is reasonable to infer that the suspect is armed and presently dangerous.)

Review Questions

1. Explain when a stop is authorized. ____________________________

____

____

____

____

2. Give an example of when a stop is authorized. _________________

____

____

____

____

3. Does information from an anonymous caller justify a stop? Name a case that supports your position. ______________________________

____

____

____

____

4. Does the officer have to give facts that support his or her argument that criminal activity was afoot (the situation looked suspicious)? Explain your answer. Can you name a case that supports your position? ____

____

____

____

5. What are a few factors that can be used to support an officer's belief that a stopped subject is armed and presently dangerous?

____

____

____

6. Describe a frisk. ______________________________

____

____

____

7. Explain the "Plain Feel" law. ______________________

____

____

____

8. When is a search warrant required? ________________

____

____

____

____

9. Is there a time limit on a stop? Is there a case that answers this question?

____

____

____

____

10. Does the officer have the authority to order the driver to get out of a car without a reason? ______________________________

____

____

____

11. Does an officer have the authority to order the passengers to get out of a vehicle?

____

____

____

12. Are there legal cases that answer questions ten and eleven? Explain.

____

____

____

13. During a traffic stop, does an officer have the authority to seize everybody in the vehicle? Is there a case that answers this question? ______________________________

____

14. When does an officer have the authority to frisk a vehicle?

____

____

____

____

____

Notes

Date:

Notes

Date:

Notes

Date:

Notes

Date:

Notes

Date:

Notes

Date:

Notes

Date:

Chapter 7

Search Warrants and Plain View

Objectives:

The student will be able to

1. identify the grounds for which a search warrant will issue,
2. identify the procedures for obtaining a search warrant,
3. identify the elements of a complaint for a search warrant,
4. identify the procedures for executing a search warrant,
5. identify the procedures for searching premises with a warrant, and
6. recognize the plain and open view doctrines.

Searches are governed by the fourth Amendment.

> The right of the people to be secure in their persons, houses, papers, and effects, against unreasonable searches and seizures, shall not be violated, and no Warrants shall issue, but upon probable cause, supported by Oath or affirmation, and particularly describing the place to be searched, and the persons or things to be seized.[167]

Notice that the Fourth Amendment requires, for the issuance of a search warrant, (1) probable cause, (2) oath or affirmation, (3) a description of the place to be searched, and (4) a description of the person or things to be seized.

Also, the Fourth Amendment protects people from unreasonable searches.[168] Recall that Katz was protected while inside a telephone booth and talking on the telephone.[169] In *Katz*, the Supreme Court ruled that the officers needed a search warrant before they could tap the phone line and listen to Katz conversation.[170]

---

[167] U.S. Const., amend. IV.
[168] *Katz v. United States,* 389 U.S. 347 (1967).
[169] *Id.*
[170] *Id.*

Grounds for which a Search Warrant will Issue

The Fourth Amendment sets the minimum standards for the issuance of a search warrant. Some states have enacted statutes that include the minimum requirements for the issuance of a search warrant. For example, Illinois enacted 725 ILCS 5/108-3:

> Grounds for search warrant. (a) Except as provided in subsection (b), upon the written complaint of any person under oath or affirmation which states facts sufficient to show probable cause and which particularly describes the place or person, or both, to be searched and the things to be seized, any judge may issue a search warrant for the seizure of the following:
>
> (1) Any instruments, articles or things designed or intended for use or which may constitute evidence of, the offense in connection with which the warrant, is issued; or contraband, the fruits of crime, or things otherwise criminally possessed.
>
> (2) Any person who has been kidnaped in violation of the laws of this State, or who has been kidnaped in another jurisdiction and is now concealed within this State, or any human fetus or human corpse.[171]

In short, a search warrant will issue when an officer submits a written complaint, showing probable cause of finding something illegal (or evidence of a crime), to a judge. (The thing or person to be seized and the place to be searched have to be described with particularity; in other words, described with as much detail as possible.)

Procedures for Obtaining a Search Warrant

Because of the fourth amendment, a search warrant requires (1) oath or affirmation, (2) probable cause, and (3) a good description of the person or things to be seized and the place to be searched.[172] Illinois adds an additional requirement; the complaint (this is the request) for the search warrant must be in writing.[173]

---

[171] See 725 ILCS 5/108-3 (quoting P.A. 89-377, eff. 8-18-95) (The statute is not quoted in its entirety.).

[172] U.S. Const., amend. IV.

[173] See 725 ILCS 5/108-3 (quoting P.A. 89-377, eff. 8-18-95).

The Elements of a Complaint for a Search Warrant

As mentioned before, in Illinois, the elements of a complaint for a search warrant are

(1) the complaint must be in writing and under oath,
(2) the probable cause must be included in the complaint, and
(3) the complaint must describe with particularity (with detail) the person or things to be seized and the place to be searched.[174]

These are the elements of a complaint for a search warrant in Illinois. (The elements might be different in other states.)

The Procedures for Executing a Search Warrant

The procedures for executing a search warrant will vary from state to state. For example, Illinois enacted a statute (725 ILCS 5/108-6) that outlines the procedures for executing a search warrant.

> The warrant shall be executed within 96 hours from the time of issuance. If the warrant is executed the duplicate copy shall be left with any person from whom any instruments, articles or things are seized or if not person is available the copy shall be left at the place from which the instruments, articles or things were seized. Any warrant not executed within such time shall be void and shall be returned to the court of the judge issuing the same as "not executed".[175]

So, in Illinois, there is a time limit for the execution of a search warrant, 96 hours. Additionally, a copy must be left with a person from whom the things were seized (or left at the location, if no person is available). And if the warrant is not executed within 96 hours, then it has to be returned to the court.[176]

Procedures for Searching Premises with a Warrant

Before entering the property, absent the legal exceptions, officers are supposed to knock and announce the search of the premises. There are situations

---

[174] *Id.*
[175] See 725 ILCS 5/108-6 (quoting Laws 1963, p. 2836).
[176] *Id.*

when officers are allowed to make entry without "knocking and announcing" the search." Some states have written statutes that authorize police officers to make entry without "knocking and announcing." For example, Illinois enacted 725 ILCS 5/108-8.

> Use of force in execution of search warrant.
>
> (a) All necessary and reasonable force may be used to effect an entry into any building or property or part thereof to execute a search warrant.
>
> (b) The court issuing a warrant may authorize the officer executing the warrant to make entry without first knocking and announcing his or her office if it finds, based upon a showing of specific facts, the existence of the following exigent circumstances:
>
> > (1) That the officer reasonably believes that if notice were given a weapon would be used:
> >
> > > (i) against the officer executing the search warrant; or
> > >
> > > (ii) against another person.
> >
> > (2) That if notice were given there is an imminent "danger" that evidence will be destroyed.

The Supreme Court stated that it is up to the states to determine when police officers (for safety reasons or the protection of evidence) should not "knock and announce."[177] The Supreme Court acknowledged that there are situations where knocking and announcing would place people in danger.[178] At the same time, the Supreme Court stated that police officers are not allowed to completely do away with the "knock and announce" rule.[179] To elaborate, if the officer can point to specific facts (for example, the suspect has access to firearms and has discharged the same during altercations) that will justify not "knocking and announcing," then the officers will be justified in dispensing with the "knock and announce" requirement. (Notice that the officer has to articulate facts.)

---

[177] *Wilson v. Arkansas,* 514 U.S. 927, 927-931 (1995).
[178] *Id.*
[179] *Id.*

Once inside the property, police officers are only allowed to search the areas that are specified in the warrant. For example, if the warrant specifies a search of the first floor, then all the other floors are off limits.

Additionally, police officers are allowed to search containers and places that are large enough to hold the item that is listed in the search warrant.[180] This means that if the police officers are looking for a rifle, then the police officers may not look inside a salt shaker—the rifle cannot fit inside the salt shaker. Moreover, once the police officers seize all the items that are listed in the warrant, the search is over—officers must stop the search.[181] To be clear, once the police officers seize all the items that are listed in the search warrant, the police officers must stop the search.

The Plain View Doctrine

While conducting a lawful search, police officers are allowed to seize illegal items that are in plain view. There are three requirements for the plain view doctrine:

1. the officer is standing in a lawful position,
2. the officer can readily grab the item, and
3. the illegality of the item is immediately apparent.[182]

For example, if the police officers are executing a search warrant and they see—without manipulating any objects—an assault rifle on the living room couch, then the weapon is in plain view because (1) the officers have a legal right to be inside the property, the officers have immediate access (they can readily grab the item) to the firearm, and (2) the criminal nature of the item is immediately apparent.

Suppose, that while on foot patrol, a police officer—standing on the sidewalk—observes, through a living room window, two sawed-off shotguns. Because the officer has a lawful right to be on the sidewalk, part one of the test is met. The officer cannot readily grab the items because they are inside a house; part two of the test is not satisfied. The criminal nature of the items is immediately apparent; part three of the test is satisfied. The items are not in plain view; part two of the test is not satisfied. Absent exigent circumstances, a warrant is required.

---

[180] *United States v. Ross,* 456 U.S. 798, 820-21 (1982).
[181] *Horton v. California,* 496 U.S. 128, 141 (1990).
[182] *Coolidge v. New Hampshire,* 403 U.S. 443 (1971).

Michigan v. Summers[183]

As Summers was walking down the steps from his house, police officers approached Summers and asked for his assistance in gaining entry to Summers's house. Thereafter, after gaining entry, Summers was seized while the police officers searched the house. The police officers found narcotics and, after ascertaining that Summers owned the house, arrested Summers for the narcotics.

After the formal arrest, the police officers searched Summers's person and found heroin. Summers argued that the heroin that was found on his person should be excluded from evidence because the police officers had no right to detain him while the search of the premises was conducted. Put another way, if the police officers would not have detained Summers, the officers would not have found the heroin on Summers' person. And the trial court agreed with Summers and excluded the evidence. (Eventually, the case reached the Supreme Court.)

The Supreme Court stated that Summers was definitely seized. Additionally, the court reasoned that the seizure did not amount to a formal arrest (the seizure occurred in Summers's house, there was no trip to the police station, and there was minimal embarrassment to Summers). In other words, the Supreme Court declared that the seizure was similar to an investigatory detention (a *Terry* style stop).

Furthermore, the Supreme Court elaborated that the existence of a search warrant shows that a neutral judge was convinced that criminal activity was present at the location of the search. Based on this, the court stressed that a person's connection to the place to be searched served as justification for a detention. Put another way, this means that if a person lives at the location to be searched, then the police officers are justified in seizing that person

In short, the Supreme Court ruled the detention of Summers justifiable because of the existence of a search warrant. (Police officers are allowed to seize people who are on the property) Based on this, because Summers's seizure was legal, the heroin found on Summers's person, through a custodial search, was admissible evidence; the heroin was used against Summers.

---

[183] *Michigan v. Summers,* 452 U.S. 692 (1981); see *Muehler v. Mena,* 544 U.S. 93, 99 (2005) (The Supreme Court allowed the handcuffing of all the occupants of the house; the search involved drugs and a wanted gang member.).

Conclusion

Searches with search warrants are preferred over warrantless searches. And probable cause is required for a search warrant. There are situations when it is not practical to get a search warrant (e.g. emergencies). These situations will be discussed in chapter eight. Additionally, searches based on valid consent are allowed. (Searches based on consent will be discussed in chapter nine.)

Review Questions

1. On what grounds will a search warrant issue? ________________

____

____

____

2. Identify the procedures for obtaining a search warrant. _________

____

____

____

____

3. Identify the elements of the complaint for a search warrant. _____

____

____

____

____

4. Identify the procedures for executing a search warrant in Illinois.

____

____

____

____

5. What is the standard of proof that is needed for a search warrant?

____

____

6. Identify the procedures for searching premises with a search warrant. ____

____

____

____

7. If the search warrant lists a large screen television, then where may the police officers search?

____

____

8. Explain the plain view doctrine. ____________________________

____

____

____

9. Give an example of an illegal item that meets the plain view test.

____

____

____

____

10. While executing a search warrant, are officers allowed to seize (detain) people who are on the premises? Is there a case that supports your position?

____

____

____

Notes

Date:

Notes

Date:

Notes

Date:

Notes

Date:

Notes

Date:

Notes

Date:

Chapter 8

Impounding, Inventorying Property, and Searching for Property

Objectives:

The student will be able to

1. recognize when impoundment/inventory of property is authorized,
2. identify the procedures for the inventorying of property,
3. recognize when a search in hot pursuit is authorized,
4. identify the procedures for conducting a search of the premises,
5. recognize when an emergency search is authorized, and
6. identify the procedures for conducting an emergency search.

There are situations when getting a search warrant is not practical. So, there are exceptions to the search warrant requirement. Additionally, the police officer will have to impound or inventory the seized property. Additionally, the officer should be aware of the situations when emergency and hot pursuit searches are allowed.

Situations when the Impoundment or Inventorying of Property is Authorized

Some laws allow for the impoundment of vehicles that are used in certain offenses (e.g. driving under the influence, possession of illegal drugs, and driving with a suspended or revoked driver's license).[184] Also, in some cities, vehicles may be towed because they are illegally parked. As long as the impoundment is legal and the police department has an inventory procedure (for the contents of the vehicles) in place, the police officers are allowed to do an inventory search of the vehicle for three reasons:

1. to protect the owner's property,
2. to protect the officers against false claims of theft,

[184] For example, see 625 ILCS 5/11-208.7.

3. to look for dangerous items (e.g. bombs).[185]

Any evidence that is discovered during a valid inventory search is admissible evidence. The evidence can be used to charge a person with a crime.[186]

Procedures for the Inventorying of Property

Police officers have to be familiar with their department's procedures for the inventorying of property. A department might have a standardized form where the officer lists all the property that is found inside the car; after the property is documented on the form, the property is removed from the vehicle for safekeeping.[187]

Hot Pursuit and other Exigent Circumstances

There are going to be situations when it is not practical to get a warrant. Due to safety concerns or the need to protect evidence officers will need to make a warrantless entry into the property. The Supreme Court has recognized four situations that amount to exigent circumstances:

1. hot pursuit of a fleeing felon,
2. imminent destruction of evidence,
3. the need to prevent a suspect's (probable cause to arrest) escape, or
4. risk of harm to police officers or other people (inside or outside the dwelling).[188]

The Supreme Court ruled that a subject is not allowed to defeat an arrest by retreating into his or her house.[189] So, if police officers attempt to arrest a subject and the subject runs inside his or her house, then, according to the "hot pursuit"

---

[185] *South Dakota v. Opperman,* 428 U.S. 364, 369 (1976) (The Supreme Court articulated the three reasons why inventory searches of automobiles are justified. Additionally, the court stressed that police officers have a caretaker role—to protect property.); *Colorado v. Bertine,* 479 U.S. 367, 371 (1987) (The Supreme Court stressed that probable cause is not needed to vehicular inventory searches; the Fourth Amendment is not implicated.); *Florida v. Wells,* 495 U.S. 1, 4-5 (1990) (The Supreme Court held that some type of departmental policy is required. In other words, if there is no policy in place, then the search (especially the opening of containers that are inside the car) might be unconstitutional.).

[186] *Opperman,* 428 U.S. at 366 (Marijuana was found in the car; the owner of the car was charged with possession of marijuana.); *Bertine,* 479 U.S. at 369 (Illegal drugs were found in a backpack that was inside a vehicle; the owner of the vehicle was charged with possessing the drugs.).

[187] *Id.* at 366.

[188] *Minnesota v. Olson,* 495 U.S. 91, 100 (1990).

[189] *United States v. Santana,* 427 U.S. 38, 42 (1976) (In this case, the subject retreated to her house and the police officers entered the house and arrested the subject. The Supreme Court said that this was a "hot pursuit" case.).

doctrine, the police are allowed to enter the house and search for the subject to make the arrest.[190] Also, an emergency search is authorized when there is a risk of harm to police officers or to other people. For example, a dangerous person who has just committed a robbery runs inside a house; there is a need for the police officers to secure the subject—to prevent the subject from hurting someone.[191]

The Emergency Search Procedures

When police officers enter a house to look for a dangerous person (e.g. armed robber), they are allowed to look for the suspect.[192] Additionally, if the officers suspect that the subject is armed, then the officers are allowed to search the premises for weapons until the suspect is secured.[193] Once the emergency of securing the subject is over, absent other justifications, and the area within reaching distance of where the subject was secured is searched,[194] the authority to search for weapons or evidence ends.[195] (The authority to search the reaching distance of where the subject was secured will be discussed in chapter nine.)

The Protective Sweep

While inside the house, if the police officers have a reasonable belief—based on articulable facts—that there is an accomplice inside the property who poses a danger to the police officers, then the police officers are allowed to search the premises for other people.[196] (This is a search for people. So, opening small drawers, small cabinets, shoe boxes and so on is not allowed.) Again, this is a cursory search for people only. (But remember the plain view doctrine. If a police officer has the authority to open a closet to look for people, and the police officer observes suspect cocaine in the closet without further intrusion, then the suspect cocaine falls under the plain view doctrine and can be legally seized.)[197]

---

[190] *Id.*
[191] *Warden, Maryland Penitentiary v. Hayden,* 387 U.S. 294, (1967).
[192] *Id.* at 298-299.
[193] *Id.*
[194] *Chimmel v. California,* 395 U.S. 752, 763 (1969) (The right to search the reaching distance of where the arrestee was secured is automatic; there is no justification needed.).
[195] *Hayden,* 387 U.S. at 299; *Mincey v. Arizona,* 437 U.S. 385 (1978) (The Supreme Court ruled that a search, after the emergency was over, was unconstitutional.).
[196] *Maryland v. Bui,* 494 U.S. 325, 336-337 (1990).
[197] Revisit the plain view doctrine in Chapter Seven.

Review

<u>Objectives</u>:

1. When is the inventorying of the property that is inside an impounded vehicle authorized?

- The inventorying is authorized when the impoundment is legal and the department has established guidelines for the inventorying and safekeeping of the property.

2. Identify procedures for the inventorying of property.

- Police officers have to be familiar with their department's procedures for the inventorying of property. A department might have a standardized form where the officer lists all the property that is found inside the car; after the property is documented on the form, the property is removed from the vehicle for safekeeping.[198]

3. Recognize when a search in hot pursuit is authorized.

- The Supreme Court ruled that a subject is not allowed to defeat an arrest by retreating into his or her house.[199] So, if police officers attempt to arrest a subject and the subject runs inside his or her house, then, according to the "hot pursuit" doctrine, the police are allowed to enter the house and search for the subject to make the arrest.[200]

---

[198] *Id.* at 366.

[199] *United States v. Santana,* 427 U.S. 38, 42 (1976) (In this case, the subject retreated to her house and the police officers entered the house and arrested the subject. The Supreme Court said that this was a "hot pursuit" case.).

[200] *Id.*

4. Identify procedures for conducting a search of the premises.

➢ Officers are allowed to look inside the premises for the person whom they are trying to arrest. If the subject is suspected of having weapons, then the officers are allowed search for weapons and secure the same. Once the subject is secured and no other justifications to search exist. The authority to search ends; further searching requires a warrant.[201]

5. Recognize when an emergency search is authorized.

➢ An emergency search is authorized when there is a risk of harm to police officers or to other people. For example, a dangerous person who has just committed a robbery runs inside a house; there is a need for the police officers to secure the subject—to prevent the subject from hurting someone.[202]

6. Identify the procedures for conducting an emergency search.

➢ When police officers enter a house to look for a dangerous person (e.g. armed robber), they are allowed to look for the suspect.[203] Additionally, if the officers suspect that the subject is armed, then the officers are allowed to search the premises for weapons until the suspect is secured.[204] Once the emergency of securing the subject is over, absent other justifications, and the area within reaching distance of where the subject was secured is searched,[205] the authority to search ends.[206]

---

[201] *Hayden,* 387 U.S. at 299.
[202] *Warden, Maryland Penitentiary v. Hayden,* 387 U.S. 294, (1967).
[203] *Id.* at 298-299.
[204] *Id.*
[205] *Chimmel v. California,* 395 U.S. 752, 763 (1969) (The right to search the reaching distance of where the arrestee was secured is automatic; there is no justification needed.).

Notes

Date:

[206] *Hayden,* 387 U.S. at 299.

Notes

Date:

Notes

Date:

Notes

Date:

Notes

Date:

Notes

Date:

Chapter 9

Consent Searches, Custodial Searches, and Automobile Searches

Objectives:

The student will be able to

1. recognize when a consensual search is authorized,
2. identify the procedures for conducting a consensual search,
3. recognize when a search incident to an arrest is authorized,
4. identify the procedures for conducting a search incident to an arrest,
5. recognize when a warrantless search of a motor vehicle is authorized,
6. identify the procedures for searching an automobile without a warrant, and
7. identify the role of a state's attorney or city attorney in the warrant authorization process.

A police officer is allowed to perform searches of premises, automobiles (a legal stop is required), and persons based on consent.[207] So, with "proper consent voluntarily given," the police officer does not need to get a warrant; and probable cause is not needed.[208] Because the state has the burden of proving that consent was voluntarily given, it is a good idea to get the consent in writing.[209] And the totality of the circumstances will determine whether consent was voluntarily given.[210] Also, during a valid vehicular stop (e.g. a nonfunctioning headlight), a police officer is allowed to search the vehicle based on valid consent.[211] Additionally, a police officer is allowed to search the arrestee's person and the immediate area in which the arrestee was secured.[212] This absolute right does not

[207] *Schneckloth v. Bustamonte,* 412 U.S. 218, 219 (1973) (The Supreme Court stated that a search based on consent requires neither probable cause nor a warrant.); *Zap v. United States,* 328 U.S. 624, 628 (The Supreme Court ruled that the Fourth Amendment rights may be voluntarily waived.).

[208] *United States v. Matlock,* 415 U.S. 164, 165 (1974).

[209] *Schneckloth,* 412 U.S. at 248.

[210] *Id.* At 248-249.

[211] *Id.*

[212] *Weeks v. United States,* 232 U.S. 383, 392 (1914) (Police officer have the right to search the person of a lawfully arrested subject.); *Agnello v. United States,* 269 U.S. 20, 30 (1925) (The Supreme Court restated that police officers

apply to automobiles. If the arrestee was an occupant in an automobile, then the police officers does not have the automatic right to search the passenger compartment of the vehicle.[213]

Also, related to searches, if police officers have probable cause to search a vehicle that is in motion, then a search warrant is not required. The police officers are allowed to stop the vehicle and perform a search based on probable cause.[214]

When a Consensual Search is Authorized

The consent to search has to be voluntarily given. The prosecutor has to prove that the consent was voluntarily given and not obtained through coercion or duress.[215] (For these reasons, it is a good idea to get the consent in writing; most police departments have preprinted consent to search forms.) Additionally, the consenter has the authority to limit the scope of the search.[216] And the consenter may revoke the consent.[217] The test for the scope of the consent is what a reasonable person would understand the scope to be based on the exchange of words between the police officer and the citizen.[218]

Additionally, regarding consent, the person must have apparent authority to consent to the search.[219] In other words, the police officer must reasonably believe that the consenter has the authority to consent to the search.[220] A hotel clerk does not have the authority to give a police officer the consent to search a hotel guest's room.[221] A landlord does not have the authority to consent to a search of a tenant's living quarters.[222] To repeat, the police officer has to determine who has authority to grant the consent to search.

---

have the absolute right—no justification is needed—to perform custodial searches.); *Chimel v. California,* 395 U.S. 752, 762-763 (1969) (Police officers are allowed to search the immediate area of where the arrestee was secured; the immediate area is also called the "wingspan" area and the "grab and reach" area.).

[213] *Arizona v. Gant,* 556 U.S. 332 (2009) (The Supreme Court ruled that the search of an automobile, in which the arrestee was a recent occupant, is no longer automatic; a search is still allowed based on other grounds. See Chapter Eight.).

[214] *Carroll v. United States,* 267 U.S. 132 (1925).

[215] *Schneckloth,* 412 U.S. at 248-249.

[216] *Florida v. Jimeno,* 500 U.S. 248, 252 (1991).

[217] *Id.*

[218] *Id.* At 250.

[219] *Illinois v. Rodriquez,* 497 U.S. 177, 186 (1990).

[220] *Id.*

[221] *Stoner v. California,* 376 U.S. 483 (1964).

[222] *McDonald v. United States,* 335 U.S. 451, (1948).

The Procedures for Conducting a Consensual Search

As mentioned before, the police officer must have "proper consent voluntarily given," for a warrantless search.[223] So, there are a few steps that the police officer should follow when conducting a consensual search:

1. get consent from a person who has a reasonable expectation of privacy,[224]
2. if more than one person has a reasonable expectation of privacy (e.g. husband and wife or joint tenants), everyone who is present must consent—if one person does not consent, then the police officers are not allowed to search,[225]
3. stay within the scope of the consent (e.g. if consent is specifically given to search only the first floor, then the officers should only search the first floor), stop the search if the consent is revoked,[226] and
4. use a consent to search form (The state and the police officers have to prove that valid consent was given.).[227]

If the court determines, based on the totality of the circumstances, that valid and proper consent was not given, then the search will be invalid.[228]

---

[223] *Matlock,* 415 U.S. at 165.

[224] *Katz,* 389 U.S. at 350 (People who have a reasonable right to privacy are protected from unreasonable searches and seizures.); *Schneckloth,* 412 U.S., at 219 (A search based on consent does not violate the Fourth Amendement; in other words, a person is allowed to waive his or her Fourth Amendment rights.).

[225] *Georgia v. Randolph,* 547 U.S. 103, 121-123 (2006).

[226] *Jimeno,* 500 U.S. at 252.

[227] *Schneckloth,* 412 U.S. at 248.

[228] *Schneckloth,* 412 U.S. at 248-249.

When a Search Incident to a Lawful Arrest is Authorized

As mentioned before, when a lawful arrest is made, a search of the arrestee's immediate area is allowed.[229] This is an absolute right; there is no justification needed. (The officer does not have to explain why he or she performed the search.) The automatic right to search based on a lawful arrest does not apply to automobiles.[230] (Police officers are still allowed to search automobiles based on other grounds; the search of an automobile requires an explanation.)[231] Some states have written the right to search in a statute. For example, Illinois enacted 725 ILCS 5/108-1.

> Sec. 108-1. Search without warrant.
>
> (1) When a lawful arrest is effected a peace officer may reasonably search the person arrested and the area within such person's immediate presence for the purpose of:
> (a) protecting the officer from attack; or
> (b) preventing the person from escaping;
> (c) discovering the fruits of the crime; or
> (d) discovering any instruments, articles, or things which may have been used in the commission of, or which may constitute evidence of, an offense.
>
> (2) (Blank).
>
> (3) A law enforcement officer may not search or inspect a motor vehicle, its contents, the driver, or a passenger solely because of a violation of Section 12-603.1 of the Illinois Vehicle Code.[232]

Again, a lawful arrest is required for the right to automatically search the subject. (A temporary detention—a *Terry* Stop—does not give the police officer the automatic right to search the subject.)

---

[229] *Weeks v. United States,* 232 U.S. 383, 392 (1914) (Police officer have the right to search the person of a lawfully arrested subject.); *Agnello v. United States,* 269 U.S. 20, 30 (1925) (The Supreme Court restated that police officers have the absolute right—no justification is needed—to perform custodial searches.); *Chimel v. California,* 395 U.S. 752, 762-763 (1969) (Police officers are allowed to search the immediate area of where the arrestee was secured; the immediate area is also called the "wingspan" area and the "grab and reach" area.).

[230] *Arizona v. Gant,* 556 U.S. 332 (2009) (The Supreme Court ruled that the search of an automobile, in which the arrestee was a recent occupant, is no longer automatic; a search is still allowed based on other grounds. See Chapter Eight.).

[231] *Id.*

[232] 725 ILCS 5/108-1 (source: P.A. 93-99, eff. 7-3-03).

Procedures for Conducting a Search Incident to an Arrest

Based on a lawful arrest, a police officer is allowed to

1. search the person of the arrestee,
2. search the immediate area in which the arrestee was secured, and
3. inspect the property that is on the arrestee's person.[233]

These searches are allowed to ensure that the arrestee is not carrying a weapon that he or she can use to hurt someone or to escape.

Searching a Motor Vehicle Without a Warrant

With probable cause, police officers are allowed to search—without a warrant—a motor vehicle that is in motion.[234] For example, if the police officer has probable cause to believe that the vehicle contains cocaine, then the police officer is allowed to stop the vehicle and search any part of the car that can conceal the cocaine. In contrast, if the police officer has probable cause to believe that there is an illegal rifle in the automobile, then the police officer is allowed to stop the vehicle and search the areas that can conceal a rifle. Containers—suitcases, purses, bags, and so on—that are large enough to hold the item of the search may be searched.[235]

Additionally, a motor vehicle may be searched, under the inventory search exception.[236] Furthermore, police officers may search a vehicle based on consent.[237] And if the police officer reasonably believes that, after a valid arrest of the driver, that the vehicle contains evidence of the crime of the arrest, then the police officer is allowed to search the automobile for the evidence.[238]

---

[233] *Weeks v. United States,* 232 U.S. 383, 392 (1914) (Police officer have the right to search the person of a lawfully arrested subject.); *Agnello v. United States,* 269 U.S. 20, 30 (1925) (The Supreme Court restated that police officers have the absolute right—no justification is needed—to perform custodial searches.); *Chimel v. California,* 395 U.S. 752, 762-763 (1969) (Police officers are allowed to search the immediate area of where the arrestee was secured; the immediate area is also called the "wingspan" area and the "grab and reach" area.).

[234] *Carroll,* 267 U.S. at 161-162.

[235] *Wyoming v. Houghton,* 526 U.S. 295 (1999).

[236] See Chapter Eight.

[237] *Schneckloth,* 412 U.S., at 219 (A search based on consent does not violate the Fourth Amendement; in other words, a person is allowed to waive his or her Fourth Amendment rights.).

[238] *Arizona v. Gant,* 556 U.S. 332 (2009) (The Supreme Court ruled that the search of an automobile, in which the arrestee was a recent occupant, is no longer automatic; a search is still allowed based on other grounds. See Chapter Eight.).

Procedures for Conducting a Warrantless Search of an Automobile

As discussed before, under an exception to the warrant requirement, police officers are allowed to conduct warrantless searches of vehicles:

1. based on probable cause and the car is mobile,[239]
2. based on consent (written consent is better),[240]
3. after the arrest of the driver, there is a reasonable belief that the vehicle contains evidence of the crime of the arrest,[241]
4. based on the caretaker function (For example, the vehicle is at a repair shop and the police officer has reason to believe that there is a firearm inside the automobile.),[242] and
5. based on the inventory search exception. (The police department should have an established procedure for conducting inventory searches.)[243]

The police officer should always be able to explain why the vehicle was searched.

The State's or City's Attorney Role Regarding a Warrant Authorization

Some police departments require that the complaint for a search warrant be reviewed by the state's attorney; in some departments, a complaint for a search warrant might require the review of a city's attorney; the attorney will provide the officer with guidance on the complaint. If the state's or city's attorney does not approve the complaint, then the police officer should follow the procedure of the department for the rejection of the complaint.

---

[239] *Carroll,* 267 U.S. at 161-162.

[240] *Schneckloth,* 412 U.S., at 219.

[241] *Gant,* 556 U.S. at 343-344.

[242] *Cady v. Dambrowski,* 413 U.S. 433, 441 (1973).

[243] *South Dakota v. Opperman,* 428 U.S. 364, 369 (1976) (The Supreme Court articulated the three reasons why inventory searches of automobiles are justified. Additionally, the court stressed that police officers have a caretaker role—to protect property.); *Colorado v. Bertine,* 479 U.S. 367, 371 (1987) (The Supreme Court stressed that probable cause is not needed to vehicular inventory searches; the Fourth Amendment is not implicated.); *Florida v. Wells,* 495 U.S. 1, 4-5 (1990) (The Supreme Court held that some type of departmental policy is required. In other words, if there is no policy in place, then the search (especially the opening of containers that are inside the car) might be unconstitutional.).

Review

<u>Objectives</u>:

1. Recognize when a consensual search is authorized.

- The consent to search has to be voluntarily given. The prosecutor has to prove that the consent was voluntarily given and not obtained through coercion or duress.[244] (For these reasons, it is a good idea to get the consent in writing; most police departments have preprinted consent to search forms.)

[244] *Schneckloth,* 412 U.S. at 248-249.

2. Identify the procedures for conducting a consensual search.

- The police officer must have "proper consent voluntarily given," for a warrantless search.[245] So, there are a few steps that the police officer should follow when conducting a consensual search:

   A. get consent from a person who has a reasonable expectation of privacy,[246]

   B. if more than one person has a reasonable expectation of privacy (e.g. husband and wife or joint tenants), everyone who is present must consent—if one person does not consent, then the police officers are not allowed to search,[247]

   C. stay within the scope of the consent (e.g. if consent is specifically given to search only the first floor, then the officers should only search the first floor), stop the search if the consent is revoked,[248] and

   D. use a consent to search form. (The state and the police officers have to prove that valid consent was given.)[249]

---

[245] *Matlock,* 415 U.S. at 165.

[246] *Katz,* 389 U.S. at 350 (People who have a reasonable right to privacy are protected from unreasonable searches and seizures.); *Schneckloth,* 412 U.S., at 219 (A search based on consent does not violate the Fourth Amendement; in other words, a person is allowed to waive his or her Fourth Amendment rights.).

[247] *Georgia v. Randolph,* 547 U.S. 103, 121-123 (2006).

[248] *Jimeno,* 500 U.S. at 252.

[249] *Schneckloth,* 412 U.S. at 248.

3. Recognize when a search incident to an arrest is authorized.

➢ When a lawful arrest is made, a search of the arrestee's immediate area is allowed.[250] This is an absolute right; there is no justification needed. (The officer does not have to explain why he or she performed the search.) The automatic right to search based on a lawful arrest does not apply to automobiles.[251]

4. Identify the procedures for conducting a search incident to an arrest.

➢ Based on a lawful arrest, a police officer is allowed to

A. search the person of the arrestee,

B. search the immediate area in which the arrestee was secured, and

C. inspect the property that is on the arrestee's person.[252]

---

[250] *Weeks v. United States,* 232 U.S. 383, 392 (1914) (Police officer have the right to search the person of a lawfully arrested subject.); *Agnello v. United States,* 269 U.S. 20, 30 (1925) (The Supreme Court restated that police officers have the absolute right—no justification is needed—to perform custodial searches.); *Chimel v. California,* 395 U.S. 752, 762-763 (1969) (Police officers are allowed to search the immediate area of where the arrestee was secured; the immediate area is also called the "wingspan" area and the "grab and reach" area.).

[251] *Arizona v. Gant,* 556 U.S. 332 (2009) (The Supreme Court ruled that the search of an automobile, in which the arrestee was a recent occupant, is no longer automatic; a search is still allowed based on other grounds. See Chapter Eight.).

[252] *Weeks v. United States,* 232 U.S. 383, 392 (1914) (Police officer have the right to search the person of a lawfully arrested subject.); *Agnello v. United States,* 269 U.S. 20, 30 (1925) (The Supreme Court restated that police officers have the absolute right—no justification is needed—to perform custodial searches.); *Chimel v. California,* 395 U.S. 752, 762-763 (1969) (Police officers are allowed to search the immediate area of where the arrestee was secured; the immediate area is also called the "wingspan" area and the "grab and reach" area.).

5. Recognize when a warrantless search of a motor vehicle is authorized.

- With probable cause, police officers are allowed to search—without a warrant—a motor vehicle that is in motion.[253] For example, if the police officer has probable cause to believe that the vehicle contains cocaine, then the police officer is allowed to stop the vehicle and search any part of the car that can conceal the cocaine.

6. Identify the procedures for searching an automobile without a warrant.

- As discussed before, under a few exceptions to the warrant requirement, police officers are allowed to conduct warrantless searches of vehicles:

   A. based on probable cause and the car is mobile,[254]
   B. based on consent (written consent is better),[255]
   C. after the arrest of the driver, there is a reasonable belief that the vehicle contains evidence of the crime of the arrest,[256]
   D. based on the caretaker function (For example, the vehicle is at a repair shop and the police officer has reason to believe that there is a firearm inside the automobile.),[257] and
   E. based on the inventory search exception. (The police department should have an established procedure for conducting inventory searches.)[258]

---

[253] *Carroll,* 267 U.S. at 161-162.
[254] *Carroll,* 267 U.S. at 161-162.
[255] *Schneckloth,* 412 U.S., at 219.
[256] *Gant,* 556 U.S. at 343-344.
[257] *Cady v. Dambrowski,* 413 U.S. 433, 441 (1973).
[258] *South Dakota v. Opperman,* 428 U.S. 364, 369 (1976) (The Supreme Court articulated the three reasons why inventory searches of automobiles are justified. Additionally, the court stressed that police officers have a caretaker role—to protect property.); *Colorado v. Bertine,* 479 U.S. 367, 371 (1987) (The Supreme Court stressed that probable cause is not needed for vehicular inventory searches; the Fourth Amendment is not implicated.); *Florida v. Wells,* 495 U.S. 1, 4-5 (1990) (The Supreme Court held that some type of departmental policy is required. In other words, if there is no policy in place, then the search (especially the opening of containers that are inside the car) might be unconstitutional.).

7. Identify the role of a state's attorney or city attorney in the warrant authorization process.

- Some police departments require that the complaint for a search warrant be reviewed by the state's attorney; in some departments, a complaint for a search warrant might require the review of a city's attorney; the attorney will provide the officer with guidance on the complaint.

Conclusion

The police officer should always be able to articulate why a search was conducted. For a search warrant, the officer has to explain the probable cause to search—in writing—on the complaint. As discussed earlier, for stops and frisks reasonable suspicion is required. This means that the officer has to articulate the factors that justified the stop and the frisk—if a frisk was conducted. This book gives an overview of Criminal Procedure the Investigatory Process which comprises a good part of what police officers do while on patrol. (There is a second part of Criminal Procedure; it is called the Prosecutorial Process, this is a topic for another book.) Lastly, good luck to you and your future endeavors.

Review Questions

1. When is a consensual search authorized? ____________________

____

____

____

2. What are the procedures for conducting a consensual search? ____

____

____

____

3. What is the scope (limitations) of a consensual search? _________

____

____

4. Can a landlord who does not have a privacy interest in a dwelling give valid consent to search the dwelling? ___________________

____

5. Can a hotel clerk who does not have a privacy interest in a room of the hotel give valid consent to search the room? _______________

____

6. Describe when a search incident to a lawful arrest is authorized. __

____

____

____

Review Questions

7. What may an officer search after a lawful arrest is made? _______

____

____

____

8. When is a police officer allowed to search the arrestee's vehicle?

____

____

____

____

9. What amount of evidence is required to stop a vehicle and perform a warrantless search of the same? _______________________

____

10. What are the procedures for conducting a warrantless search of a vehicle? _______________________________________

____

____

____

11. What is the state's attorney or city's attorney role in the warrant authorization process?

____

____

____

Notes

Date:

Notes

Date:

Notes

Date:

Notes

Date:

Notes

Date:

Notes

Date:

Notes

Date:

Index

www.ingramcontent.com/pod-product-compliance
Lightning Source LLC
LaVergne TN
LVHW070952210926
848482LV00002B/187